Praise for
Hiding in the Light

"Rifqa Bary's story is a powerful testimony to standing for the truth in the face of many difficulties and tall odds. In the words of this young woman who has already been through so much, we are painted a picture of stark cultural contrast—that of slavery and liberty, duty and love, and bondage and freedom. As much as anything, this is a story about the first freedom upon which America was built—the freedom to believe and live one's life according to those beliefs. Rifqa's inspiring story reminds us why we must continue to stand for faith and freedom!"

—TONY PERKINS, president of Family Research Council

"Rifqa Bary's story unveils God as the Father to the fatherless whose pursuit of His children is fiercely beautiful. Once I started reading, I couldn't put it down. She invites readers to walk beside her on her fascinating road and to see the God she saw when she said her very brave yes to Jesus."

—SARA HAGERTY, author of *Every Bitter Thing Is Sweet*

"An extraordinary glimpse into the faith of a Christ-follower and the sovereignty of God. Rifqa's story informs, inspires, and empowers."

—MAX LUCADO, pastor and author

"This is truly an inspirational story of a young Muslim girl's journey into the arms of Jesus and the discovery that Jesus is everything that she had been looking for. Her heartbreaking journey is hard to fathom, and yet her suffering was the one thing that led her to Jesus. This story will give you not only insight into what it means for a Muslim to convert to Christianity and the heavy price associated with that, but also the importance of Christians breaking through the stereotypes and reaching out to Muslims in love."

—NAGHMEH ABEDINI, wife of imprisoned pastor Saeed Abedini

"Not only does Rifqa Bary's story bring to light key tenets of Islam we so need to understand, it will show you the courage true faith provides. This is a book you will finish in a hurry, as you'll want to know what happens next! Thank you, dear Rifqa, for counting all as loss for the sake of our Savior."

—KAY ARTHUR, cofounder of Precept Ministries International and author of *When the Hurt Runs Deep*

"Enrapturing heart and spirit, Rifqa masterfully shares insights into immigrant Muslim life, tearing the veil of mystery with the power of the gospel. Although chronicling her own account, her words echo the cries of young Muslim women worldwide, and manifest on each page is the signature of our sovereign God. Rifqa's story is authored by Jesus—come read what He's written."

—DR. NABEEL QURESHI, best-selling author of *Seeking Allah, Finding Jesus* and speaker with Ravi Zacharias International Ministries

"I hope you can feel the gentleness of Rifqa's heart as I did when I read her story—I love it! In my own experience as a child, I had hidden in a cocoon of despair and lived with the brutality of loneliness—I understand how she felt. When you give your heart to Jesus Christ, you have to be brave. I was so touched by the sadness and the joy of someone who never denied Jesus."

—NICKY CRUZ, evangelist and author of *Run, Baby, Run*

"Rifqa is my hero, and this book details her amazing story never before told in its entirety. Even though it was all over the national news, if you thought you knew what really happened—think again. I stayed up all night reading this book. *Hiding in the Light* is a testament to what happens when one ordinary person is touched by the one extraordinary Savior of the World."

—JOHN STEMBERGER, president and general counsel, Florida Family Policy Council

HIDING
in the
LIGHT

RIFQA BARY

Why I Risked Everything
to Leave Islam *and* Follow Jesus

HIDING
in the
LIGHT

WATERBROOK
PRESS

To my precious baby brother, Mohamed Rajaa Bary.

I can only imagine the unanswered questions that may plague you. Why did the big sister you adore leave you and never come home again? My hope is that this book is a long letter explaining why.

Although you may never understand my answer, my prayer is that the words bound within these pages allow your heart to heal. My prayer is that one day you will forgive me for the pain I have caused you. I left not because I did not love you enough. I left because I encountered a God who was worthy of forsaking all . . . even the most prized little man in my life.

If only you could peer through my dreams and see how I ache to hold you in my arms like I did so many years ago . . . but this time I never let you go.

Author's Note

In 2009–2010 my story broke in national and international media. As often happens, many of the news reports centered on speculation and untruths. This book fulfills my desire to give an accurate account of my personal experiences within my family and community. Please understand it is not my intention to malign Muslims or Islam.

Though the story contained in these pages is true, I have changed the names of many individuals for reasons of privacy and safety.

HIDING
in the
LIGHT

Prologue

The mosque discovered my secret.

And now my parents knew it too.

The cover of early morning darkness was fast slipping away. Mom was still sleeping. Dad had cut his trip short and was on his way home. I had to get out of there *now* to survive. It was the only way I could escape the penalty, not for any crime I'd committed but for what I believed.

I wrote with trembling hands in those final, desperate moments, inches before sneaking from my bedroom to the front door and out into the unknown:

> *Jesus Christ is my Lord and Savior. I refuse to deny*
> *Him, nor will I ever. I pray and hope you find His*
> *mercy and forgiveness. Love you both dearly.*
> *—Rifqa*

I took one last look over the room that had been my refuge. I propped the note on my pillow, whispered a breathless goodbye, and was gone.

What I was running away from was certain.

But what I was running toward . . .

God only knew.

One

M y skin shone like caramel in the summer sun as I played in the garden outside our home in Sri Lanka. Honeysuckle sweetened the air. I drew in a breath and let it fill my lungs, small as they were. I was only five, such a little girl in a world so big, yet I felt carefree and safe. Joy bubbled within me. I raised my arms and imagined them as wings. I was a mighty bird drifting across the cloudless sky. Running in circles with my wings spread full, I gasped, laughed . . .

And then stood still.

For in that moment I felt something strange and new. A Presence, quiet and comforting, hovering, nearly tangible. It pressed in closer and closer.

I had never experienced anything like this before. But I wasn't scared. I felt strangely protected, cherished, even loved. Peering closer toward what seemed to be its direction, I half-expected to see the empty air staring back at me with noticeable face and features. Instead I saw nothing. But I knew *Someone* was there, a strong Man who seemed to stir the breeze as He moved. Too visceral to be invisible.

Goose bumps broke out on my skin, and powerful excitement filled my tiny frame. Resuming my play, I looked back, still expecting to see a physical person. Again there was no one. I laughed. It became a game. Play, turn back, giggle. Play, turn back, giggle. This Presence was so enticing, so warm. I didn't want our time to end.

And even when it did, somehow I knew He would come back again.

I was a happy little girl growing up in Sri Lanka, especially when I was with my mother, my "Mummy." I always wanted to be by her side. Her big, beautiful smile warmed me, and her hearty laugh echoed throughout the house.

If I close my eyes, I can still picture her in the long cotton gown she wore at home, remembering how she tried to get me to eat when I was very young. I reached for her long, curly black hair, teasing her with my mischievous eyes.

"One more bite, little Rifqa," she said in Tamil, our native language.

Opening my mouth wide, I let her feed me with her hands. I savored the taste—rice balls flavored with curry.

"Okay. Let's make this one an airplane! Open wide, Rifqa!"

Mummy's plane delivered its payload. I chewed open-mouthed and let out a squeal. She made meals fun, knowing it was the only way she could get me to eat. Airplane after airplane flew across the table and into my mouth.

Back then my mother occasionally spoiled me when Daddy was out of the house. Sometimes she let me try on nail polish, even though my Muslim family did not allow me to wear it because they say it makes us unclean. But she let me keep a stash that I would hide and then wear when no one could see. I knew once I was old enough to pray, I would not be allowed to use it anymore. Still, I would never forget the twinkling of my fingernails in the dim light of my room.

Early memories of my dad aren't as easy to recall. But I do know I adored him. I thought he was *huge*! I now realize his height is average, but back then he was the biggest person in my little world, which made me believe he was safe and would keep me out of harm's way. I loved his attention whenever I could get it, and more than anything, I ached to be special to him—like a prize he would forever treasure.

My father supported us by selling gemstones, often to dealers in America. It was not unusual for him to be away for months at a time on business. I didn't understand as a child why he was gone for so long, but I remember my joy when he returned. Once when he came home after one of his lengthy trips, he looked different. His normally clean-shaven face was dark and fuzzy. I reached up to feel his cheek, then put my own cheek against his prickly face, squealing with delight. Instead of running away, I rubbed my other cheek against his and shrieked some more. He smiled at my fascination with his beard.

Over the next few years he frequently brought me clothes or candy from his faraway travels. Though I delighted in those, the real treats for me were the rare times he stayed home for more than a few days in a row. Those were the times when we could all be together.

Despite being gone often, my dad was a faithful leader at our mosque. It was both his honor as a man and his duty as a Muslim. Just as I was born Rifqa Bary, just as I was born Tamil, I was also born a Muslim. Of course I was too young to understand, at five, what Islam really meant for me and the people around me, but it was quite clear that this was who we were, what we would always be. The strict Muslim culture was all I had ever known, so I accepted it as normal. Every person and every day belonged to Allah. That's just the way it was. Who would ever feel the need to question something so settled and certain?

My devout family followed all the required rituals of Islam: the five daily prayer recitations, the fasting and feasting, the memorization of the Qur'an. Some of my earliest memories involved getting up at three or four in the morning during the holy month of Ramadan, eating a meal before sunrise that my mother had prepared, then going back to bed, under orders to say a special, memorized prayer that I recited to myself as I tried drifting back off to sleep. By as early as age seven, I was expected to participate in the all-day fasting—no food at all, not even a drink of water—until seven or eight at night when we were allowed to break our fast with some dates as well as a Sri Lankan soup my mother made every day for the occasion.

I also remember the Imam coming to our house each week. Even though he taught me to "read" the Holy Book, I had no idea what any of it meant. I spoke Tamil and a little English, but I couldn't read in either language. The Qur'an is written in Arabic, and to translate it is considered unholy by the Muslim leaders where I grew up. We only had to be able to quote from it—perfectly, in Arabic—to earn the approval of our elders and the mosque leaders.

But although its language and mystery was a source of great confusion to me, my father's praise made all the hours spent studying worth it. I tried for his sake to be a good student of Islam, as did my big brother, Rilvan.

Rilvan is two years older than I, so our relationship (like most siblings who are similar in age) swung wildly between close friendship and red-faced hatred. He was my closest companion, and I loved him dearly, even if I wouldn't admit it then. I would shadow him around the house until he finally snapped in annoyance, and I would run away only to return undaunted. When he was in a more tolerant mood, we would play tag and run around the house together, shouting and laughing, taunting and teasing.

One day shortly after my sixth birthday, my father returned home from a business trip with a little metal airplane he'd been given at the airport. Rilvan was playing with it, and I demanded a turn with it too.

"No, Rifqa," he said. "Daddy gave it to *me*. You can play with it later."

"Let me see it!" I shouted. "Just for a minute!" I said, before unsheathing my secret weapon. "I'll tell Mummy!"

"No," said Rilvan, hugging the plane to his chest.

"Mummy, he's—"

"All *right*," Rilvan said, groaning and heaving the airplane straight at me.

I remember seeing it cruising toward me, but after that things are a blur. All I remember is the blood. So much blood, everywhere, running down my face, soaking my orange dress. My mother, hearing my cries, rushed at me from another room, while Rilvan stood silently, horrified, staring in disbelief at his hands, like, *How in the world? All I did was*—

Time felt like it had stopped. In fact, the last sight engraved on my memory that day was the hands on the clock, each pointing straight up, exactly 12:00 noon . . . before my world went pitch black.

What happened next was a swirl of detached, floating images, weaving into and out of themselves in waves of trauma and consciousness. I remember hearing my grandfather's voice: "Help! Somebody please help!" I remember the faint, frantic echoes of doctors and nurses, one of them, I guess, announcing to my family, "We cannot take her here, I'm sorry. Her wound is too serious. She's bleeding too much. You'll need to take her to the other hospital that can perform the kind of surgery she needs. But hurry! She might not make it if you don't get her help right away!" I ached for my mother's comforting presence. Limp and lifeless, I lay in my grandfather's arms, moaning for breath.

Not till several days later would I fully recover my senses. All but one. My right eye, so badly damaged from the metal plane's sharp edge, would never respond to the various surgeries and treatments they employed in hopes of restoring its function. Despite weeks in the faraway hospital, under the care of its supposedly more highly trained staff, my sight in that eye failed to return. It never has. Its caramel brown color faded to a milky gray.

But as distressing and disorienting as my partial loss of vision proved to be—gone at only six years old—the oddest loss came from somewhere else, somewhere equally (if not more) unexpected.

From that point forward, I felt as if I had been marked. I couldn't quite wrap my head around it, but something had changed. As soon as we returned from the hospital, my family began to treat me differently. When they looked at me, the warmth in their eyes would cool. Where before they would laugh at my stubbornness or persistence or whatever, now they would much more likely chide me to behave myself and keep quiet.

Why? I wondered. I mean, it's not like my injury had crippled me. I'd been able to adapt and adjust and pretty much do everything I could do before. I was still the same Rifqa, I knew. But their behavior toward me had changed all the same. They seemed to feel that I had become a burden. It was as if every time they looked into my blemished face, they saw something in me they just couldn't acknowledge.

In any case, even the most minor mishap or demand of mine could now invoke their sharp anger, resulting in serious consequences. Although physical discipline was common in my culture, I hadn't witnessed it in my own family until this time. I remember clinging to my mother's skirt hems one afternoon, begging her to play with me. I must have whimpered one time too many, because she finally just snapped. With a jerking lunge, she scooped me up and threw me. I crashed down on the cold concrete floor, scraping my knees and banging my elbows.

"Stop it!" she screamed. "I do *not* have time for you today, Rifqa. Go!"

At first I craved her attention more and more. But as the bruises and the shouting matches began to increase, I started to hide from her. Her rage would surface without warning, and if I did something she didn't like or took too long to finish my chores, I could expect a stern reprimand. Even accidentally spilling milk or something would earn me a stinging cheek. There was no denying the growing hardness in my mother's heart.

I remember finding a stray kitten, for example, roaming around our neighborhood. He was gray and covered in white splotches, and his eyes would shine brightly when he craned his neck to look at me. I named him Ajay. He limped on his back left leg and would tense up whenever I touched him, so I could tell he had been abused or neglected somehow. I held him for hours and hours in the yard, trying to imagine why anyone would abandon him. He was so friendly; he couldn't have possibly meant anyone any harm. He just wanted attention . . . and maybe a bit of milk. Whatever happened, I was intent on keeping him alive. I was the only one who could.

Every day I brought him a bowl of milk because my parents wouldn't let him inside. They told me he was unclean, like so many other things were, and wouldn't even allow me to touch him in their sight. I offered to give him a bath if he was so unclean. But they said that wasn't what they meant.

"It's ugly, that thing," Mummy would say. "It could have rabies. We don't know. Just . . . just leave it alone, Rifqa. Leave it where it is."

One morning, however, my mother's mind seemed to change toward Ajay. We were leaving for the market when she said I could bring the kitten along. I was ecstatic. Finally, I had worn her down! I scooped up Ajay and climbed into the yellow rickshaw my mother had chartered.

The ride was boring but the market was grand. There were more tents and pavilions than I could count, and the air was thick with merchants crying their wares and with shoppers trading gossip. Every now and then a breeze would stir up a little column of road dust that would tumble down the aisles, as if it were shopping as well. The gathering was large but well-tended to. Tall palm trees lined up like armed guards behind the endless rows of shops, and low shrubs fenced in the area from the nearby highway. Ajay recoiled against me when we first came upon the crowd, but as we wandered through the market, he eventually poked his head out to investigate the savory smells and strange noises, to which he added his own mewling. My mother walked beside me without saying a word. She consulted her list and methodically found our groceries.

We completed our shopping and walked back to the waiting fleet of taxis and rickshaws, carrying our parcels, Ajay at our heels. But Mummy's eyes, I could see, were like stones for some reason. She was tired, impatient, and strained. Then, suddenly, with one frustrated sigh, she stomped on the ground as hard as she could, trying to scare the cat away. Ajay stiffened, arched his back, and darted into the tall grass by the road. Gone. It was the last I ever saw of him.

I stood there in shock, staring into the empty air. Why? Why would my mother do that? But with no other word of explanation, she grabbed me, swung me up roughly into the rickshaw, and motioned for the driver to take off.

"Rifqa," she said. "I told you not to go near that thing. I let you play with it all afternoon, but that's enough. It's gone. We're leaving."

The memory of that day burned into my mind, as it probably would into yours, not only because of my heartbreak at losing Ajay, but because, in a certain way, the image fits my mother (and my father) so perfectly. Voices stern and eyes void of emotion, their message self-evident: *Go away, go away, go away.*

It was another early lesson in life. My family was not to be trusted.

When I was about seven or eight, a distant uncle came to my house to watch me one day while my mom and brother left to go somewhere. He had dark skin and jet-black hair that was always gelled to the side. His almost black skin seemed darker against the white shirt he was wearing. The stench of his body odor filled the room.

I was uncommonly small for my age. And my uncle, perversely recognizing the contrast in our strength and size, took advantage of my inability to defend myself and sexually violated me that day. Even though I didn't understand what was happening, the ordeal made me feel disgusting. I knew better than to cry. I wanted to be strong. But I felt weak and scared. Something inside me died that day.

The next time my parents sent me back to be watched by him, my uncle told me he would kill me if I ever told anyone what he had done. I believed him, yet I couldn't stand carrying this secret. I didn't want to ever be left alone with him again, so I later told my mother what happened. But rather than comfort or defend me, as I'd hoped or expected, she simply started wailing with grievous tears, "Don't tell your father! Don't tell anyone!"

My father found out anyway. And he was enraged. But not so much at my uncle. In some Muslim cultures, like mine, this kind of violation is a great source of dishonor. Yet the shame is not attached to the abuser; it is cast on the victim. So not only was I viewed now in my parents' eyes as a half-blind picture of imperfection, but I was also a shameful disgrace to the Bary name. My mere presence and appearance were a stain against the most important thing of all—our family honor.

In this way, I was sort of like the kitten. Dirty. Devalued. Unclean. And in my naive mind I wondered if I, too, would be chased away. I could only guess at what would ultimately become of me, because we never talked about this episode or my feelings again. We simply ignored it and moved on.

Literally.

Two weeks later my father announced that we would all be going with him the next time he left for America.

This sudden change of plans took our tight-knit community by surprise. In the following weeks our home was filled with a rotating circle of friends, acquaintances, and other well-wishers, all of whom exhibited varying degrees of curiosity. My parents were well-regarded at the mosque and around the town, and their abrupt interest in emigration struck many of our neighbors as suspicious. Mummy and Daddy wore guarded smiles all through those weeks, embracing their friends a bit too tightly and laughing at their jokes a bit too loudly. They told me to keep to myself and not bother the grownups, but I understood what they really meant, the subtle, underlying message. They worried I might say something embarrassing. About my uncle? I didn't know. I never really knew. But better to keep quiet. I understood that much, loud and clear.

Actually my parents might have been right to worry about the impression they were giving their neighbors. Some people just couldn't resist the potential for gossip. Our more inquisitive visitors, with perfect nonchalance, oblivious to the social discomfort they created, would wonder aloud about our reasons for leaving.

"For Rifqa," my father would reply, when pressed to explain. "Better hospitals in America. Better surgeons too." He would look at me, warning me with his eyes. "If we can't find help for Rifqa there, we won't find it anywhere."

That couldn't have been the real truth, however. The last doctor to examine my blinded eye had frowned and told us that beyond some cosmetic corrections and other procedures to prevent pain and infection, there was very little that medicine could do for me in my home country or any other. But the word *America* seemed to hold some sort of bewildering power over people that allayed further questions.

We were leaving.

That was all.

So we left for the United States in 2000 on a temporary visa, though my father's plans in moving were never temporary. We ended up staying without the necessary legal paperwork after the visa expired.

As for me, I'd lost so much of myself in those first few years of life, I didn't really mind leaving my homeland behind. I remember watching out the window of the airplane as my island grew smaller and smaller, swallowed up by the ocean's waves and the coming night.

I never returned to Sri Lanka. And I don't think I ever returned to being a child.

Two

My first impression of New York was its startling lack of palm trees. Those aren't the only types of trees in Sri Lanka, of course, but they litter the beaches so densely, their sheer abundance had caused me to barely even notice or think of them. That is, until suddenly in New York, I realized there were none. Anywhere.

The only things that seemed to grow in New York City were skyscrapers, giant sentinels standing on every street corner. Sure, trees and grass could be found in the city parks. Here and there a pitiful weed might sprout from a crack in the sidewalk. But those were rare splatters of green in a vast sea of gray.

Yet even though the city seemed drab and unnatural, I found myself enjoying my first weeks in America. Just the diversity of people here was amazing! White people, black people, plus a whole lot of other people whose skin was some shade in between. Poverty was prevalent, as it had been in Sri Lanka. But everything else seemed prevalent too. I might see people dressed in suits and fancy dresses, or was just as likely to see someone walking around in a clown costume or a policeman's black-and-blue uniform.

And if all this diversity had any one thing in common, it was this: they were all in a very, *very* big hurry.

We soon settled into life as New Yorkers, living in very crowded, very minimal conditions. Our little house in Queens, as I recall, consisted of just two rooms. Not much to see, no place to spread out. But this was America—that magical word, that magical world—and just being here, just living here, meant more to us than most Americans can probably imagine.

My father, almost immediately upon our arrival, was typically gone from home again, just like before (which we all began to prefer), and my mother was often busy doing her own things. So I was forced to become a very independent child for an eight-year-old. Every morning I woke up on my own and got ready for the day. I walked to school by myself, sixteen blocks that slowly morphed from lower-class suburb to urban sprawl. It was a twenty-minute walk, but I often found myself making it in as little as fifteen, due to my sometimes frantic pace. I wanted to be brave and confident, but it was hard not to be afraid of the homeless men who shared the sidewalks in early morning Queens. I would hold my breath, hoping no one would approach me. And whenever anyone looked at me for too long, my feet would move faster of their own accord. If the smell of cigarettes or body odor ever drifted noxiously toward me, my chest would tighten and I would gasp and sweat until I was safely around the next corner—away from any memory of my uncle's foul scent.

My parents had wanted to send us to a Muslim school, but they couldn't afford it. Our budget could only cover public school, although according to my father, there was no Allah in public school. Yet without much choice financially, my parents enrolled us in the nearest school and trusted my brother and me to see to ourselves, taking care of things like homework and attendance on our own.

I had been a somewhat gifted student in Sri Lanka, but American school was a whole different planet. There were dozens of classrooms with students of all colors, both boys and girls in every class. The teacher would lead us through the Pledge of Allegiance each morning, which I tried to learn while standing awkwardly with my hand across my chest. Even the bathrooms were exotic to me, their glorious privacy maintained by individual stalls that surrounded each toilet. Wow! I'd never seen anything like it.

Despite my broken English and my unfamiliarity with American ways, I was not a complete social failure. I managed to make a few friends, even though I was not allowed to go to their homes. Rilvan, of course—a boy—would spend late nights at his friends' houses almost every week. But me, I spent every Friday night staring at the same square of ceiling above my bed.

My parents were not blind to this double standard, but they would scold me for pointing it out. "You are a girl," my mother would say, "and girls stay at home." Rilvan would be a man someday, she told me, and he needed to be able to function freely. The place for women was at home, close to their families, close to Allah.

Close to suffocating.

I was occasionally allowed to invite friends over to our house, but I never felt comfortable bringing them into the tense atmosphere. I was afraid of being embarrassed by my parents.

For example, my friend Emma lived next door. She brought over a backpack full of Barbie dolls one afternoon for us to play with. I was in awe, not only at being able to hold one of these dolls that I'd never owned but always wanted, with their pale skin, rosy cheeks, and light brown hair, just like Emma's, but also at how many of them and how many outfits Emma pulled from her case. I had never seen so much fun stuff in one place at any one time. It was more toys than I owned. We spread out the dolls and the accessories on the front steps of my house. Emma taught me how to play dress-up, and we let our imaginations take care of the rest.

We continued this way for a couple hours, it seemed, when eventually I saw my mother returning down the street. She stepped onto our walk, saw the dolls . . .

And froze.

Her jaw set into a painful-looking grimace. Then, with frightening speed, she grabbed me by the hair and dragged me into the house, but still where Emma could see and hear.

"What! Just *what* is this?" she shouted.

"We're just playing, Mummy."

Her voice continued rising, her insinuations flying. I was already burning with shame, even before she whacked me across the face with her hand. It wouldn't have been as bad if it had happened behind closed doors, where no one could see. But the look on Emma's pained face confirmed that she had watched the whole thing develop and escalate. Grabbing up her toys in haste, she ran back to her house. I put my hand to my reddening cheek and wondered what I had done so wrong.

The following school year started in August, and in no time, it was September 2001. And all of a sudden New York was the worst place on earth to be a Muslim. At school, on the street, anywhere in public, the skin on our faces and the timbre of our accents made us guilty by association with the 9/11 terrorists.

Not long after the horrific events of that day, I was outside playing alone in our tiny yard. A "Psst!" grabbed my attention, and I startled in the direction of the sound. On edge.

Not to worry. It was Emma, leaning over the fence. The tiny houses in our Queens neighborhood were packed so tightly together, like sardines, there was hardly any way to stay private, even when trying to keep to yourself.

"You wanna come over?" she whispered.

I smiled as best I could. "I don't think I should. You know . . . my parents."

She did know, of course, but she was persistent anyway. "Come on," she baited me. "We're just gonna be praying. Your parents love praying, don't they?"

To a nine-year-old this logic made sense. So we furtively ducked into her house before anyone in mine could see me.

It didn't occur to me, oddly enough, that going over to an American family's house to pray might raise issues. It had also never occurred to me that prayer was not exclusive to Islam. I had only ever seen Muslims pray, so I assumed the practices of other religions were just too alien to imagine. Not that I was totally ignorant of other religions. Even in Sri Lanka, it was nearly impossible to live in the modern world without some exposure to Christianity. But most of what I'd learned about Christians from the Imam had been in the form of warnings and lessons against things that Muslims shouldn't do. I was always taught that Christians were devils.

"Over here!" said Emma as she led me into their living room, a smile in her eyes. I envied that smile. Lately all of my smiles had seemed fake and forced. And yet here was Emma, smiling beautifully with hardly any thought or effort. I stepped up beside her, wanting to be close to my friend.

Looking around, I wasn't sure who all these people were, but they appeared to be extended family and close friends. They were forming into a sort of circle, holding hands and pleasantly talking. Emma grabbed my left hand while her mother held my right, and I was struck by a sudden serenity. Here, in this circle, I seemed to know I would be safe, even with the ramifications of my presence so nearby at my house and likely awaiting me when I got back.

As Emma's dad started to speak, everyone closed their eyes. I kept mine open, too curious to resist. I didn't understand many of the things he said, but I nodded my head anyway, like the others were doing. Then I heard him say a certain word that caused my mind to swirl, my heart to nearly explode. "Jesus," he prayed, "we ask that You would comfort . . ."

Wait! What did he say? Jesus?

Almost in echo, I could hear the Imam's voice in my head: *They're Christians!* I looked from face to face and remembered all I had been taught about avoiding people like these. I panicked.

"I'm . . . sorry," I said, blatantly interrupting. "I need to go. I just . . . Bye." And I left.

Spooked by this shocking, much too intimate encounter with Christians, I freshly devoted myself throughout the next few weeks to studying the Qur'an and the other practices of Islamic faith. Now that I was more conscious of other religions, I paid closer attention to the concept of Islam and its effect on my family.

The first thing I noticed was that whenever Daddy was home, my mother's authority disappeared. She was as subject to my father's domineering as I was. He would listen to her thoughts sometimes, and once or twice I heard him give her the honor of asking her opinion on an important decision. More often, though, he kept his own counsel, and that was it. He would do whatever he thought would keep our family afloat, and he would make sure my mother knew not to oppose him.

I remember one time when she got mad at him for something at a grocery store and then walked away from the checkout stand in anger. My father was furious that she had "shamed" him by walking away. When we got inside the car, he screamed at her for nearly forty-five minutes. He called her awful names and repeatedly told her what a disgrace she was. I wanted to get out of the car and run away from the hatred he spewed, but I didn't dare. I didn't want to be another victim of his rage.

More and more, he was becoming quick to punch or slap any of us for any reason. It wasn't necessarily for discipline, because he hit us even if we hadn't done anything wrong. All it would take was for one of us to do something he didn't like. I remember just acting silly one day (something I did frequently, but he was so rarely home that he never saw me). He grabbed me and beat me for "displeasing" him, he said. I learned the hard way that being silly—or loud—was not acceptable around my father.

Nor was needing him to care when I was upset. I recall waking up in the wee hours once, jolting awake from a particularly horrible nightmare. I was sweating and scared and couldn't go back to sleep. Rocking back and forth on my bed, I started to cry. I needed someone to comfort me, to tell me everything was okay. Clinging to my blanket and shivering, I knocked on my parents' bedroom door. My dad came out, angry that I had awakened him.

"Rifqa! What are you doing? Go back to your bed!" His harsh tone cut my heart.

"I had a bad dream. I'm scared." Tears streamed down my face.

"I don't want to hear it. Go away!" He pushed me out of the way and slammed the door in my face. Whatever comfort I thought he might've given, I realized I wasn't getting any. And whatever safety I once felt from him, it was no longer there.

Normally he didn't hit me in public. But one time when I was about nine, we stopped at a restaurant on a trip. He ordered some sort of shrimp and rice dish for me, which was allowable under our strict Islamic dietary laws, but I wasn't very hungry and the shrimp didn't taste good, so I scraped it to the side. Without warning, my father slapped me hard in the face and then said I had to eat the shrimp. Without delay, I stuffed it into my mouth.

Always best not to disagree with him.

Even Rilvan wasn't safe from the abuse. I'll never forget the day I overheard my father tearing into Rilvan's room in a violent rage, waking him from sleep, repeatedly beating him for something Rilvan had done that shamed our family. I was so scared, but again I didn't dare intervene out of fear for my own safety.

The only way I thought I could possibly please my dad was to impress him through my devotion to Islam, since being Muslim was the one thing that was most important to him. Maybe if I studied the Qur'an for hours at a time it would change his heart.

So rocking back and forth in the bedroom of my small New York home, I threw myself into memorizing it. I'd sit on the floor doing my daily recitations. "Rooobummaa Yuwaaano . . . ," I echoed. "Subhaaa Wata Allaaaah . . ." I had no idea what I was saying, but the poetic rhythm was soothing. Gaining my dad's acceptance would be even better.

Unfortunately it never happened.

Three

The boy's name was Aiden. He was about my age, maybe a year or two older. And even though his height towered over my small frame, I didn't feel uncomfortable around him, like I did around other boys, maybe because of his bright, pure eyes that settled my uneasiness. Boys—talking to boys, relating to boys—this was a big concern at our house. As a rule, I was strictly forbidden from interacting with them.

But this was different. Our dads worked together, which was the only reason Aiden and I ever got to be around each other. Occasionally my family would visit his home for our dads' business meetings. Our parents would go into a room and talk, leaving the kids to play together. My mother and father were too busy to notice the moments that Aiden and I were left alone. So in those uncommon slivers of time, I was able to come close to doing something my life rarely allowed: have fun.

Aiden's joyous laugh was contagious. "What would you like to do, Rifqa? We can play cards or hide-and-seek! Or . . . hmm . . ." Pausing, he cupped his face with his hands and sat down on his backyard bench. Without any time for me to respond he jumped and yelled, "Oh, I know! We can play tag!" Excited, Aiden stood up from the bench like he had figured out how to fly to the moon. His smooth chocolate skin and dark brown hair gleamed in the summer sun.

My response to him was silence. I probably looked unfriendly. But truthfully, I was baffled. Baffled because he had asked my opinion of what we should play. This was unheard of.

Be careful, Rifqa, I cautioned myself. *It's probably just a mean trick.*

But the peace on Aiden's face drew me toward him. It led me to trust

him. Why was he being so kind to me? He was different from the other
Muslim boys I knew.

Within the hour, my parents announced they were ready to leave, so
Aiden and I went back inside the house. I politely turned around to say
goodbye. Out of the corner of my eye, I noticed a delicate blue tapestry
hanging on the wall, the elegant script of a strange word—*Amen*—
embroidered on the wool. My eyes shot back to reread the words. I was
curious. I pulled him aside and whispered so my parents wouldn't overhear. "What does that word mean?"

"What word?" he said, confused.

"The word written on that tapestry . . . 'Amen.'"

"It's what we say at the end of a prayer."

Oh! It suddenly dawned on me. Aiden wasn't a Muslim—because the
Muslims I knew certainly didn't say "amen" at the end of their prayers. But
how could Aiden *not* be Muslim? The only boys I was ever allowed to talk
with were Muslim.

After a moment's hesitation, the words tumbled out of me. "I don't
understand. How do *you* pray?" I asked, probably more desperately than
he expected, but I was trying to rush the conversation. My heart beat
quickly with the looming fear that my parents could walk around the
corner at any moment.

"I pray like I'm talking to you right now—in English. I just talk to
God from my heart."

His words completely bewildered me. *Talk to God . . . like I'm talking to a real person? in English? from my heart?*

In my room that night, I couldn't stop thinking about what Aiden
had said. Memories drew me back to the prayer time at Emma's house
after 9/11. What Aiden said was true. Emma's family also had prayed to
God as if . . . as if they were just talking to Him. To think that someone
could pray in English about whatever they wanted to was both scandalous

and fascinating to me. In my culture, we only prayed in Arabic. I never understood what I was actually saying. And we certainly didn't pray whenever we felt like it or about whatever we wanted to tell God or ask Him. I was raised to believe that prayer was an obligatory response to a dictating God. Ten to fifteen minutes, five times a day. Each day came with specific prayer times, measured according to an Islamic calendar. And if a Muslim missed that window of time, it was too late. Too late to pray.

Nothing spontaneous or personal about it.

Unfortunately I was a bit of a carefree child, and I frequently skipped prayer times, even with my childlike hunger to earn Daddy's approval. Afterward, my parents would berate me, then push me into a room, shove a prayer mat at me, and scream at me to perform what Muslims call *selah*. Refusing to do so was not an option. A missed prayer time could technically be made up, but it definitely wouldn't reap the same blessings, they told me.

Prayer seemed like a lot of trouble for nothing.

But could it possibly be more? Really?

No, surely Aiden and Emma were deceived, I thought, *just like the Imam said all Christians were,* recalling the teaching of the mosque. You could almost feel the mockery when he said it. The small room of a dozen or more people beating their hands on the desks as the Imam said, "If Jesus is God, as Christians say, why could He not save Himself? Ha! Ha! Ha! These people are deceived, thinking a man is God. How stupid! Even a dog would know better than to believe such nonsense." People hissed and howled in agreement as our Imam stretched the ridicule even further. I had laughed too, with the rest of the crowd.

But now, in this moment, in my room, I didn't know what to believe. I just knew the two couldn't add up. And I wanted to know the truth.

There's something about the way Christians talk to their God, I remember thinking. When Emma's family prayed, I sensed an intimacy there, yet respect. And they didn't talk to God as though He were angry, but as if He were there. And open. And listening. And that He cared what they were saying. I was so intrigued by this thought. Astounded really.

Aiden's words awakened my heart and left behind a temptation to step closer and see this God for myself. Could there really be more to life than repeating unintelligible words from a book simply for the unattainable approval of my strict father? This God that Aiden prayed to—could He be the same Presence I encountered in my garden in Sri Lanka as a small child? I felt like I was groping in the mist for my answer. Yet the fogginess was becoming clearer with each passing step.

Four

As much as I was seeking truth, life forced me to go on as normal. That wasn't easy when my mind turned to the things I'd seen and been hearing about the Christian's God and how they so freely related to Him. I wasn't sure why I was so uncommonly drawn to these new, unthinkable religious concepts that kept flying at me from nowhere. The novelty of them struck me and ignited my boundless curiosity. Or maybe I was struggling to square why my friends' experiences, so drastically different from my own, seemed to result in this natural aura of peace and easy confidence. Was I crazy to wonder about it? Was I wrong to notice? Life in Aiden's home, life in Emma's home—it sure didn't feel like life in my home.

Of course, our regimented praying wasn't the only thing distinctive about my family and our faith or about the expectations placed on me as a Muslim girl. Spending as much time at home as I did, I was extremely familiar with the trajectory my parents and culture foresaw for me.

My mother, for example, like many Muslim women of her day in Sri Lanka, had been pulled out of school at fourteen so she could focus on what her father considered her chief priorities: domestic duties. Women in my culture are seen as assets mainly for their abilities to cook, clean, and bear children. My mother was no different.

And yet, to her credit, despite receiving only the educational equivalent of an American sixth grader, she learned her lessons well. She's one of the hardest-working and most brilliant women I've ever known. She taught herself English after moving to the United States. And on top of that, she taught herself the difficult intricate craft of embroidering beads onto wedding dresses, a totally new skill for her. After hundreds of hours of practice, she became an excellent seamstress. She didn't work outside of the house, but she frequently worked into the night on small projects like these.

She was also a master when it came to cooking, since she'd been practicing from the age of twelve. Every day of my childhood, I watched as she slaved in the kitchen for hours. But even though she put so much work and time into preparing our meals, we never ate together as a family. Daddy was so rarely home for dinner anyway. We dished out our own food from the big pot on the stove whenever we were hungry. Cooking wasn't a passion or a choice of hers; it was a duty of the life she was born into. The life I was born into. The life I would inherit as I came of age.

And so as I sat in my lonely room, increasingly curious and spiritually hungry, all these new thoughts of mine shared uncomfortable space with thoughts that were generations old and perhaps impossible to counteract. My life would most likely resemble my mother's in more ways than I wanted to accept.

And that thought depressed me.

When I was eleven, however, joy entered my world again.

"You're going to have another brother, Rifqa."

Mummy's long, curly hair cascaded around her shoulders as she rubbed her belly and announced the big news. I loved seeing her hair hang freely and loosely at home, not imprisoned in a *hijab* (the Muslim headscarf that surrounds the face) every time she stepped foot outside. But though my ears tingled with excitement at her surprising words, captivated at the thought, I couldn't help but detect a certain seriousness in her tone of voice, tinged perhaps with an element of fear. I stared at her, speechless, taking in the competing signals. What would this mean? I'd always been the youngest. I wasn't sure what to feel. Happy? Worried? Fun? Even further displaced?

Yet my anticipation grew as my mummy's belly did. I started dreaming about holding a baby in my arms. I internally vowed to be the best big sister I could be. And then, finally, in the middle of a particularly stormy night, my father rushed the two of them to the hospital, leaving Rilvan and me at home to await news of our brother's arrival.

In a matter of a few days, my parents walked in the door, carrying my new baby brother in his car seat. I could barely contain myself, dying to see him.

He was perfect. His tiny face. His big, bright eyes. His warm head with little strands of straight dark hair. A bundle of delight. He instantly captured my big-sister heart. My mom told me they had called the Imam in Sri Lanka and asked him to name their new son. His name would be Mohamed Rajaa Bary.

Rajaa.

He became the light in my dark little world. I fed him, played with him, bathed him, and put him to bed. I felt almost like a second mom. Even at such a young age, I was zealous to protect him from anything that might hurt him. When I was with Rajaa, nothing else mattered. He looked at me with his big brown eyes, and I felt love and acceptance that I didn't get anywhere else.

For a brief while, his presence gave me reason to be happy. Happier than I'd been in a long time.

The same year Rajaa was born, my father announced we were moving again, to Ohio. The cost of living in New York was too high, he said, and most of his travel was close to the Ohio Valley region. Plus he'd heard good things about the school systems there. Soon we were packing our little dark-green Toyota and pulling away from my Queens neighborhood. Peering behind me, I cried and waved goodbye to New York.

Daddy found us a house in Gahanna, a lower-middle-class suburb of Columbus. The neighborhood was markedly different from where we'd

been living. No noisy cars or blaring sirens endlessly whizzing by. In addition, the landscaping was much more manicured than our New York
home. It was definitely the nicest house we ever lived in. The grass was
neatly cut, and a small tree stood in the front yard. The pearl-white paint
of the home gracefully contrasted the deep-maroon door and window
shutters.

Nice.

From the outside looking in, you'd think a loving family lived inside.

You'd be wrong. My parents' erratically unpredictable tempers could
still attack at any moment, and Rilvan and I were constantly fighting.
Many of our battles were over a computer—the only one we had. I remember one event that occurred shortly after moving there. I'd been waiting all
day to play on the computer, but Rilvan wouldn't stop using it and kept
ignoring my requests.

"Come on, Rilvan. Can I use it now?"

Nothing. No answer. Purposeful silence. Again and again I asked.

Finally, angrily, I pushed his hand to get his attention. Flaring up
from his seat, he shoved me to the floor and started kicking me in the side,
the chest, the stomach. The force of his pounding feet sent shock waves of
pain throughout my body. I lay on the floor, crying, while my mother, sitting nearby with hands folded, watched everything unfold with cool indif-
ference. As if I were invisible. I simply didn't matter.

Rilvan, just like my dad, always got his way. And for one reason: because he was male. I once saw him draw a knife on my mother when my
dad was out of town, demanding that she immediately cook some dinner
for him. "Make me food, woman," he yelled, flashing the tip of his weapon
toward her.

"You're a monster! You know that?" she yelled, panicked. "Is this what
I gave birth to you for?"

But what could she do? She helplessly clattered her pans on the stovetop and began cooking. Because that's what women do. For men. When would this reality sink into my hard head?

So as I writhed in pain and cried out for help, my mother's face said it all: I deserved what I was getting for even daring to resist his male domination.

Moving to Ohio obviously hadn't changed anything.

Nothing ever would.

Living in a new state also meant starting at a new school. It didn't help matters that I was entering the awkward time of life known as the middle school years, which are stressful enough even without all the adjustments to meeting new people and encountering new environments, even without the drama playing out each day at home. It also didn't help that my new school was in the town of New Albany, which was much more affluent than Gahanna.

New Albany looked as much like a fairy tale as anyplace I'd ever been. White picket fences surrounded perfectly manicured lawns. Trendy shops and posh buildings reflected the grandeur of the businesses and wealth of the residents. I felt like an impostor walking through this flawless, affluent town. My family barely made ends meet.

As I walked up to my new school on the first day, I couldn't help but gawk at its architecture. It looked more like a mansion than a school. Regal white columns reached two stories high along the front of the massive red-brick building. I suddenly felt very alone and self-conscious, sensing a hundred pair of eyes all staring at me. I seemed to be the only brown girl in the hallway; everyone else was white. This was so different from the diverse demographic of my New York school.

As the days turned into weeks, I learned to dread lunchtime the most. Loneliness buried me as I sat by myself at a table and ate my sack lunch.

The laughter around me made me ache. I wanted so badly to fit in with the other girls. As I was already feeling hated by my family, school seemed my only hope of acceptance. And now even that didn't seem very likely.

Just as all middle schools are segregated into cliques, mine was divided by social status. It was a sort of caste system. Invisible lines clearly defined who was in and who was out. Only the rich girls sporting designer clothes made it to the upper tier. Girls like me—wearing my Walmart-brand outfits three times in a row before switching them—were ignored and cast aside as worthless.

I really struggled with the fashion thing, not by a lack of desire to express myself but definitely by religious restriction. In keeping with Muslim custom, my shoulders and legs had to be covered at all times. I could never wear any of the cute shorts or sleeveless shirts and sundresses that the other girls wore. All of my clothes were baggy and shapeless. I simply wasn't allowed to factor style into my wardrobe.

But I knew it wasn't just my clothes that made me an outsider. Even if we had money—which we didn't—my Muslim culture prevented me from doing a lot of things the other kids did. Middle school seems to be when boys and girls start to notice each other. That is, unless you're a girl being raised in a strict Muslim environment. My mother made that perfectly clear. One evening I was watching a movie in the living room as she sat next to me and worked on a sewing project. When the movie ended with the couple kissing, she looked over at the screen and howled. She began stitching more aggressively, shaking her head with the thought of her worst nightmare becoming a reality. She looked at me with a steely expression and said in Tamil, "Rifqa, don't you dare think of ever having a boyfriend. You won't have a home here if you do."

I know it may sound strange, but I was forbidden from communicating at all with non-Muslim boys, which basically meant with any boys. Not that I *didn't* talk to them. I did. At school, where my parents couldn't see. But any interactions with a boy, no matter how casual and offhand, if not with a Muslim boy who was preapproved by my parents, was sure to invite a stern scolding. In their eyes, I had no need to talk to a boy, let alone ever date one. After all, I would never be free to choose the man I wanted to marry when the time came for thinking about such things. Like the generations before me, my marriage would be arranged by my father when I reached my late teens or early twenties. And I would marry whatever man he arbitrarily chose for me, most likely someone significantly older or wealthy or a hardheaded Muslim. Or all of the above.

In my culture, if a girl were to fall in love and marry someone, she would be disowned by her entire family. Marriage was for custom, not for love. My parents married when my mom was sixteen and my dad was at least ten years older. They never met before they were married. She saw only one picture of him before their marriage, and that was all. In fact, under the even more rigid structure of her own upbringing, she wasn't even allowed to show her face to men. My parents, thankfully, weren't quite as strict as that. The mosque was the only place where I was made to wear a hijab. But marriage and restrictions on boy-girl relationships were a tradition that remained rigidly in force.

New school. New struggles. Old histories. Old oppression. Between all the rules the mosque imposed, coupled with the whiplash of abuse it created in our home—which was liable to spark at any time without warning—I began to silently question Islam. In small ways, of course, I'd been questioning it for a long time, or at least dabbling, fascinated with a God who somehow wasn't a fist of resistance, indifferent to human emotion, and impossible to please. A God who wasn't like ours.

I mean, what if God were more like the loving, graceful Presence I'd experienced as a child that day in our garden in Sri Lanka? Huge and strong, yes, but also warm and engaging? Distinct and above me, and yet desiring to relate to me? Not a heavy, threatening demand but a desirable, intimate Friend?

I don't know, maybe it was just something weird in me, all these daydreams and questions. I'd noticed, the older I got, the extent of my inquisitive nature was dialed a little higher than that of most other kids my age. I wanted to know the why behind the what. I felt as though human beings were created with an intense desire to live for something bigger than themselves. The only thing Islam left me feeling was empty and detached. It took and took and took, but rarely if ever did it give. It forced me to *do* stuff but wouldn't let me *become* anything—at least not anything I wanted to be.

Why? Why did it have to be like this?

Of course I couldn't talk about these things to anyone, because questioning the Qur'an or Islam is forbidden. It's one of the most shameful things you can do as a Muslim. But my family began to notice I was slowly abandoning my devotion to the daily practices of Islam. I really didn't care anymore. The abuse in my home had escalated to the point where I truly felt hatred toward my family. Fights with my older brother were turning more and more physical. I felt so small, so weak, so defenseless. Despite the physical pain, the pain on the inside was what hurt the most.

I loathed my life. Depression cloaked me like a dark cloud. As a twelve-year-old, some days I would look out my window, watch the cars driving past on the street, and think despairingly, *If this is all that life has to offer, I don't want to be alive. Maybe it would be better to die.*

I started to relieve my pain by using razor blades to cut myself. I would gouge at my wrist and think about how much I hated my family, how much I hated school, how much I hated the life I lived, how much I . . . hated. It was better to feel self-inflicted physical pain than to constantly ache on the inside.

I wanted more. I wanted out. I wanted answers. I wanted truth. I was sick of staying silent, just sitting there and taking it, doing whatever they said, being whomever they told me to be, reeling backward from them whenever they felt like hitting me, slapping me, degrading me for no reason. I wanted to rage. I wanted to scream. I wanted freedom in every sense of the word, in *any* sense of the word: freedom to choose, freedom from pain, freedom from a sterile, hyper-controlling system that dictated my every thought without even caring who I was. I wanted to know that someone, anyone, could hear my cries. I wanted to *want,* and I wanted someone to listen. And if they didn't, if they wouldn't, if I couldn't get anybody to care, I was done. Done with life.

I meant it.

I was only twelve years old but already torn in half. And alone in my bedroom one night, throbbing in pain from another beating, grasping to survive what my suicidal thoughts were taunting me to do, I crumpled to the floor, heavy tears smearing my face. A tingle of involuntary shame shot up my back as the cry inside me began to congeal into blasphemy. Yet I pressed into the moment, unable anymore to absorb what my life had become and was becoming. I cast it all aside in one agonizing crescendo, as I sensed the harsh carpet digging into my knees beneath me. Having nowhere else to go with my thoughts, I stared up toward heaven and said, "God! If You're there, if You're real—please!—stop *hiding* from me! I don't care if You're Allah, Buddha, Jesus—whoever You are—just show me! Because if You are the truth, I will give my life to You. I will follow You—whatever the cost.

"I'll do it!"

I let the words linger there as my exhausted emotions panted for breath. When I opened my eyes again, nothing had changed. I was still Rifqa, still hurting, still crying, still trapped in the living hell of my home, still squeezed into the same petite body. My pastel quilt was still tossed lazily over the bed, just as I had left it earlier that day. Books and clothes were still scattered and piled up on the floor.

Leaning back pitifully against the corner of my bed, I sighed with despair and disappointment. My relief apparently wasn't coming. The sky, visible through the window as I stared off into the distance, formed the perfect metaphor of my emotions. Dark, gloomy clouds mocked the sunshine I craved.

Slowly I forced myself to my feet and slid onto the bed sheets, pulling the blanket over me. Its warmth and comfort swallowed my shivering body. For now, it housed the only sense of peace I could expect from the agony in my heart. I didn't care if I ever woke up again to live my abusive nightmare.

Five

Hallway. Locker room. Lunchroom. Bathroom. Math class. Everywhere I went at the beginning of the new school year, a Korean girl with long black hair seemed to be there. We never really talked, just hellos and head nods. We didn't hang out in the same social circles. But she was remarkably omnipresent. And every time we crossed paths, something magnetically drew my spirit to her.

I followed her into our classroom one morning as the school bell was ringing. Chairs screeched backward as kids sat down. Backpacks were unzipped and zipped, and conversations hushed as our seventh-grade math teacher demanded attention. "All right, class. Settle down."

She lifted a stack of papers and passed a thick batch to the first student in each row. "I want you to partner up and do these problems together. Some of them may be challenging, but do your best. Blank sections are not acceptable."

Math is the least of my problems, I thought as I scanned the arriving page to see what kind of algebraic horrors we were in for. Students started putting desks together with their partners. I just sat there, staring at the equations, not knowing who'd want to work with me, remembering why I hated these forced teamwork assignments.

"Hey, you wanna be partners?" someone asked, boldly approaching.

Her.

The everywhere girl.

"Uh, sure," I said politely, wondering why she was crossing over to my lower social caste. Surely there were other kids she'd rather have picked. I'd never thought of myself as worthy of her notice even though I'd certainly noticed *her.*

"Okay, good!" Her chirpy voice and welcoming face startled me. "I'm Angela, by the way. Your name is Rifqa, right? Are you a Christian?"

So we're cutting right past the small talk, are we? Just like that? The stark randomness of her question caught me off guard.

And yet I didn't hesitate before answering. "Yes . . . Yes, I am." No way was I going to blow an opportunity to fit in with such a popular girl.

"Great! Do you want to come to church with me?"

Do you have any idea what you're asking? But again, the dishonest answer rolled off my tongue before I could retrieve it. I had to say *something*. But what?

"Yes. I'll come with you," I answered.

My insides lurched, knowing I was digging myself into a really deep hole. *What are you doing, Rifqa? How do you expect to get away with this? Your parents are going to be furious with you for even considering her invitation!* I knew I'd just caused a mountain's worth of trouble in the space of about ten seconds.

Lying didn't seem like such a good idea anymore. This was going to be a big mess.

Math, again, was the least of my problems.

As class dismissed, Angela asked if I wanted to meet after school to talk about going to church together. *Okay, sure.* Because even though the fear was high in me, even though I knew my parents could never know anything about it, what else was I left to wonder? The whole thing had come up in such an odd, out-of-the-blue way. What if this was what I'd been searching for? What if this was how God had decided to stop hiding from me?

What if?

The question that drew me into meeting her was, *Am I willing to find out?*

I'd told Him I'd follow Him if He stopped hiding.

So that's how, going completely out of character from my usual routine, I found myself walking through the posh neighborhood that surrounded our school that afternoon, taking Angela up on her suggestion to eat something at a nearby restaurant called the Rusty Bucket.

To most people, this place was a casual dining hangout: bar and grill food, heavy appetizers and six-dollar hamburgers, steaks and seafood. But for me it was incredible. My family never ate out, and at home we only ate familiar Sri Lankan fare. Yet here Angela and I were, children pretending to be grownups as we seated ourselves and opened the dinner menu, which was big enough to cover our small faces. All the entrées, as I scanned the selections, seemed unusual to me. I figured chicken curry probably wasn't an option.

Our server approached in a fancy white uniform, and I let Angela order for both of us, since she seemed to know what she was doing. My mind was more on what she and I were soon to be talking about. *Christians. Church.* What did those words even mean? *Should I just come out and tell her the truth about who I am? And who I'm not?*

After a few minutes of small talk, I took a deep breath and dared to say it. "Angela, I need to tell you something. I'm not a—," only to be interrupted by the server.

"Here you go, ladies," she said as she set our food on the table. "Let me know if there's anything else you need." And then she turned and walked away.

Before we started to eat, Angela looked at me with a sweet smile and asked, "Is it okay if I pray?"

I nodded and followed her lead, pretending to know what I was doing. She bowed her head slightly and closed her eyes. I quickly did the same but then peeked one eye open to see what she would be doing next. Her eyes were still closed as she started to speak her prayer, so I respectfully shut mine too. And listened. With piqued anticipation.

"Father, thank You so much for this food," she said. "Thank You for Rifqa and giving us a chance to meet. Be with us and be glorified in the things we talk about. In Jesus's name. Amen."

Amen. There it was. Simple. Genuine. I was overwhelmed. She couldn't have imagined what I was feeling. To her it was just so ordinary and everyday. Praying. But to me . . . I was reminded of Emma's house in New York when her family had prayed so openly and sincerely after 9/11. How was it possible to pray with such gratitude or such familiarity?

In that moment the guilt became too heavy to bear. I couldn't conceal it any longer. I confessed as if caught in a heinous crime.

"I'm not a Christian!" I suddenly spit out. The statement hung in the air awaiting a response from my newfound friend. I could feel my tightened shoulders slowly relaxing as the deception came to light.

She didn't respond immediately, taken aback. So I leaned in closer to fill the awkwardness, my voice dimming to almost a whisper as I said, "I'm a Muslim."

I don't know what I expected her to do or say. But not this. Her face sort of lit up with a mixture of compassionate interest and curious excitement. Without saying a word, her glowing expression seemed to tell me this news of mine was actually a welcome confession.

"Angela, I don't know how to tell you this, but I come from a *strong* Muslim family. My parents can never be allowed to know I'm even thinking about anything related to Christianity. If they were to find out I went to church with you, trust me, it would be *very* dangerous."

I paused. My face grew serious as I locked eyes with hers. "This has to be secret, okay? My parents *cannot* know about this. Do you understand?"

I didn't have to wait. Her response was automatic. "Of course, Rifqa! We'll make it a secret. I'm sure we can figure out a way."

Minutes slipped into hours as we talked. I told her about my family and the grave danger that awaited me if I went to church. I hid nothing. I shared everything. I actually couldn't believe some of the stories and details I was telling her—things I'd never told anyone before. Ever. But I'd been carrying it alone for so long, and she seemed like someone I could trust. Talking about it that afternoon felt freeing and frightening all at the same time.

I imagined, to her ears, the descriptions I disclosed of my family and situation seemed incomprehensible. My life painted such a stark contrast to the picture-perfect family life most New Albany students seemed to have. My friends at school would talk about their families, and I envied them: a loving stay-at-home mom who bakes when friends are over, a hardworking father who makes a lot of money. While most of my classmates were splurging their allowances on designer clothes and living in stately homes, my reality involved endless, heated conversations between my parents about not being able to make our rent. I would never want my friends to see my father's tyranny and how he treated my mother and us. I would never invite Angela to my house. But I could invite her to understand. And I could hope she would.

Her jaw dropped lower and lower with each revelation I delivered. Stunned disbelief. Which didn't surprise me. But if you don't come from a culture like mine, if you're a young teenager growing up in church, it's hard to fully grasp the consequences and persecution involved when a Muslim embraces Christianity. Even here, in America, the "land of the free." You may be able to empathize with some of the day-to-day dynamics of our lives, but you can't process the fact that leaving Islam will cost you everything, possibly even life itself. I'd heard stories of Muslims who'd forsaken Islam and been banished from their families, never to be heard from again. But what seemed normal to me seemed off-the-charts impossible to Angela.

So even in saying a lot, I held back from coloring this part of my tale in all its grim shades of reality. Instead, I softened the worst of it to the threat of being disowned by my family, although even this word seemed outrageous, perhaps overly dramatic to my Christian friend.

"They would really disown you?" she said.

I nodded. "Uh-huh."

"They would actually hurt you?"

I nodded again, dipping a french fry in ketchup and tearing it apart with my teeth.

"I can't believe it," she said, staring off, shaking her head, increasingly bewildered. "You can't even go to church? That is *so* wrong!"

But if her riled indignation succeeded in making the injustice sound totally appalling to her, the validation of her reaction served to truly fortify my backbone. I was growing more determined by the minute. I *was* going to church with her. Whatever it meant. And in the meantime, I wasn't going to leave here before asking her every question about Christianity I'd been harboring in my head for I don't know how many years.

"What does being a Christian mean?"

"What is the cross?"

"Why did Jesus die?"

"What do you do at church?"

"How many rules do you have?"

"What are you not allowed to do?"

I peppered them one after another, firing at will. As soon as she'd answer the first, I would impatiently let loose with the next. I was like a beggar at a banquet table, unable to stop at a single serving. Each answer unpacked a freedom in her faith that simply sounded too good to be true. Everything she said caused my aching, imprisoned heart to want more: honest openness with God, the will to choose, life with a loving community of faith. Oh, how I craved these things!

What a contrast to my Islamic society and immediate family. The Muslims I knew did everything out of obligation or compulsion. Decisions were made in accordance with the culture of honor we were forced to abide by. Shame was a forceful tactic used to push our community to follow Islam, to scare us into avoiding sin. Honor and reputation mattered most; our faith revolved around being seen by others as holy and righteous. Even my memorization of the Qur'an was mostly for the reputation of my family within the Islamic community, not for my relationship with Allah.

Angela's faith, on the other hand, was so compelling. Her heart, I could tell, was truly connected to her God. She personified freedom and grace. And meeting her that day proved to be the beginning of an upside-down, inside-out adventure that would change *everything*.

I was in for the ride of my life.

Six

I'm going to study at my friend's house after school tomorrow," I lied to my parents one Thursday night. Now that I was a little older, my parents allowed me to be out of the house a little bit, but only if it involved schoolwork (or later my job). They didn't question me this night, making the deception feel even worse. But I pushed past the queasy feelings as well as the thought of whatever consequences would result if my secret were discovered. I rationalized to myself that it would be worth it.

What Angela had described to me all sounded worth it.

So when school let out the next day, on Friday afternoon, I rode the bus home with her, in electric anticipation of what this unknown evening would hold.

Being around Angela and her family was beyond refreshing. Her house was so enormous and beautiful that I felt miniscule in it, yet the mood inside gave off such a powerful sense of peace and safety. I soaked it all up as I sat and listened to her practice her piano lesson before we left for church. Her hands seemed to dance across the keys, and the music helped me stay relaxed. I was nervous about what I was about to experience and what I would find there. It still terrified me that I was going behind my parents' back, committing the worst possible crime a Muslim could commit. But I rested my head against the wall, letting the music fade away my fears. A large brown clock hung above the piano, and in between Angela's practice pieces, I listened to the steady rhythm of the second hand pushing time forward, ever nearer to the coming hour. *Tick tock. Tick tock . . .*

Before I knew it, it was time to go.

Angela's father drove us to the church in their family van. And even with my thoughts absolutely spinning—*Am I crazy for doing this? What*

*will happen if my family finds out? Could this really be the thing I'm
searching for?*—I couldn't believe how safe I felt with him, especially having only just met him. I'd always assumed every man was like my father.
Cross, short-fused, volatile, irritable. But Angela's dad was different. The
light in his gentle eyes beamed with kindness and meekness. And his love
for his daughter, just as her adoring love for him, shone through in their
comfortable interaction.

The relationship they shared caused my heart to burn with a sad jealousy. I thought of all the years I'd tried to win my father's affection only to
consistently come up short. The hours I would pour into the Qur'an never
seemed to be enough. I could never attain his standard of loyalty to Islam.
I'd come to the point where instead of trying to please him and win his
heart, I'd simply given up. Enough was enough. I'd closed off all emotion
toward him, receiving the beatings and quietly accepting his control and
criticism, yet boiling with hatred inside at the power he wielded over my
life. As I noticed in Angela and her dad how different it could actually be
when a father cares so deeply for his child, the disparity between our two
lives pierced my heart like a dagger. I wanted to cry because of how warm
I felt with this stranger.

But the pain only further confirmed my decision as we pulled into the
church parking lot and I swung out of my seat onto the faded asphalt.
"Have a good time, you two," her dad said as Angela leaned in to exchange
a quick, private conversation with him in Korean. I could tell she'd already
told him about my family situation, and the look on his face as he waved
goodbye assured me of his love, hope, and fatherly concern for my good.

I knew full well the step I was taking as I walked toward the church
building, my reflection staring back at me from the glass doors. My thick
dark hair was piled into a neat bun, and I donned a small yet hopeful
smile. As Angela opened the door for me, my silhouette separated into
two, and she motioned with her head for me to walk in ahead of her. I
obeyed and glided forward.

Many smiling faces greeted us as we entered, each of them looking like Angela with beautiful dark hair and almond-shaped eyes. Excusing herself for a moment, she scurried ahead to meet with a small group of people, huddling into a makeshift circle as she spoke, I assumed, about me. She looked like a coach before a game, giving the team specific instructions, then asking if there were any questions. She was talking in Korean, so I wasn't sure what she was saying. But every so often one of the girls would look in my direction, then turn back and nod in agreement and understanding. An excitable "aah" and "ooh" would arise from the group as I gazed awkwardly into the air, not knowing exactly what to do, feeling so out of place. But as they peeled off, one by one, from their impromptu round table, walking toward me with hands outstretched and cheerfulness in the faces, I melted at the gentleness of their love.

"Unbeliever in the house," they'd apparently been told.

Guess it brings out the hospitality in people.

Not wanting to be rude but having risked everything to come see what the inside of a church looked like, I was able to lose myself behind the girls' conversations with their other friends to wander off and explore the place alone. I took in every detail of my surroundings. I recall particularly feeling lured toward a lineup of hand-drawn pictures hanging in a hallway. They'd obviously been sketched and colored by little kids, and one of the drawings seemed to leap for my attention from the plain white walls. I slowly whispered its words as I read—"Jesus loves me"—and reached forward to touch the inscription on the paper.

I was full of questions. And maybe the one I asked myself while marveling at this picture summarized them all. How could a child be convinced that a prophet (which I understood Jesus to be) actually *loved* her?

What an odd statement to write, I thought.

Jesus loves me?

To a lot of people, the words "Jesus loves me" sound as fundamentally fixed in time and space as two plus two or Isaac Newton's laws of motion.

But hearing them for the very first time, I huffed to myself in denial. *Love doesn't really exist! It's just a fairy tale that's only lived out in movies.* Yet, deep down, something in me wanted to think that a kid who could write and believe this idea on a piece of construction paper might actually be able to live and experience it in real life.

Maybe even a kid like me.

"Come on, Rifqa! Worship is starting!" Angela appeared, tugging at my arm and leading me toward the sanctuary. The enticing melodies of a guitar grew louder as we approached. Entering, we walked into a large meeting space, its lights dimmed just enough for me to make out the arrangement of the room. *Where am I?* was my immediate first impression. This was a completely different world than anything I'd ever seen. It was certainly nothing like a mosque! Men and women in the same room? The women not wearing anything to cover their heads? And the music . . .

It was breathtaking.

This first, official physical contact with Christianity defied everything that had been knit into my DNA as a Muslim child. Especially, I think, the music. I had always been told that singing anything other than the Qur'an was *haram* ("sinful"). Only holy chants were allowed. So I was not expecting the heavenly sound of these worship songs. Beautiful, yes, but . . .

Should I be here? Should I have done this? Shame and embarrassment reached down and cloaked me like a shroud. The keen awareness of what my parents would think of this dishonoring act, mingled with the sudden, overwhelming explosion of sights, sounds, and experiences that raked across my ingrained sensibilities of what constituted appropriate reverence—my heart didn't know where to file all the things I was feeling.

As the worship music echoed in my ears, I thought of my own experiences of Islamic worship. My mind instantly raced back, remembering a warm breeze coming through the open window of our car as I rode with my father on a summer day in Ohio. Arabic praise blasted through our radio speakers, recognizable phrases that had been as familiar to me in my childhood as the alphabet. Men chanting "Laaaa illaaha illulaaaaa" ("There is no deity but Allah"), accompanied only by the leathery pounding of a *djembe* drum, rang through the car. It reminded me of chanting I'd heard as a little girl in Sri Lanka, singing along proudly for my father to hear.

"Why is there only a djembe beat?" I asked. "Why don't they use more instruments?" It seemed drab compared to the American music my friends listened to.

"Only natural instruments like the djembe are used," my father told me. "Everything else is dishonoring to God. And only the Qur'an can be sung," he adamantly added. "Nothing else!" I gazed at him from my seat in the car, his face beaming. Pride and honor affirmed his righteousness as he sang along with the words that were so familiar in tone yet totally devoid to me of any meaning.

As this memory dissolved, reality yanked me back to Angela's church, where the united flow of worship filled my ears and thirsty soul with a new sense of guarded delight.

So this is how Christians worship . . .

I felt like I was in heaven.

Even in the dimmed lighting, I could tell that everyone was deeply engaged with the service. And the more familiar and acclimated I became with what to me was a completely new dynamic, the more I began to bask in the safety and peace surrounding me. I had never felt such a palpable sense of acceptance and belonging, drawn into an unseen current toward a spiritual destination that I dearly wanted to reach and experience.

Fighting not to stare or accentuate my foreignness, yet still looking around in wonderment, I fixed on the sight of an old, wrinkled woman standing nearby, singing and weeping. The expression on her face was so precious, so beautiful as she poured out her heart to the One she loved. The words "Holy is the Lord" shone in reverse type on the black screen at the front of the sanctuary, and she sang them as if nobody else was in the room. I kept sneaking glances in her direction, watching in awe the joy she expressed, my heart pounding, wanting badly to find the peace she displayed as she sang with certainty and conviction. Profound trust and confidence. She inspired me so much that, in a rush of unfiltered desire, I dared lifting my hands with the rest of the congregation, since this seemed to be the posture of choice in the room, yet I had no idea what I was doing or saying. I was feeling it, wanting it. Maybe, in one way, I was reaching for an answer I so desperately wanted to find. Could my hands somehow touch the face of the One who enchanted this woman so?

After a while the worship music ended and the speaker stepped forward to speak. *What was he going to say?* I wondered as we all sat down. I wiped my sweaty palms across my jeans, wishing to calm my nerves as I braced for this new part of the service, having finally gotten used to what had been happening up until then. I hung on his every word, listening for something that would truly click, something that would help me make sense of this odyssey, the spiritual trek that had finally led me to this place, to this moment. Somehow I knew he would form a sentence or express a truth that would clear up my questions and lead me to answers.

But it all seemed like a bunch of stray thoughts jumbled together. I couldn't make sense of anything he said. As someone starting from such a childlike point of inexperience, I had no frame of reference, despite wanting to understand him so badly. How ludicrous it all seemed. *And did the speaker just say this man named Jesus . . . is God?*

Skepticism kept racing into my mind, even as eagerness fought hard to displace it. Yet the one thing I couldn't shake, no matter how unintelligible his words, was this: As a child, I had fully given myself to Islam, to Allah. Islam was my life, my family's life. And despite taking it more seriously than just about anybody I knew, my heart now felt as lifeless as a corpse. My only solace was in sleeping, where the pain and agony couldn't actively plague me. Something needed to change. I knew that much to be true.

Perhaps Christianity wasn't the answer.

But Islam surely wasn't.

The speaker—a man Angela called "pastor"—after wrapping up his short talk, invited anyone to come forward for prayer who wanted to. I wasn't really sure what this meant. Going forward? To pray? And yet as others began slipping out of their seats and edging down toward the front, I strangely felt the tips of my toes aching to join them.

What a feeling! Everything around me seemed to disappear in that moment: Angela and her posse of friends, my own fears and hesitations, the withering stare of my father. This was life and death. Desperate hunger. Was there any truth at that altar? My life depended on what I might find there.

I wanted to go get it and nothing was going to stop me.

It all happened fast. My mind pushed away all rationality, knowing the shame of what I was contemplating, that it could never be reversed, that I was defying the honor of untold generations in my family line, which would never be the same again. These grave consequences gave way in my mind to a steely determination and a tangible sense that the God of the universe, and maybe even this man called Jesus, truly did love me.

I stepped into the aisle as if drawn by powerful arms, holding me in all my pain and brokenness. His presence was the only power holding me together. I felt like I was breathing pure strength, a sheer sense of confidence that everything would be okay. The only time I remembered ever feeling anything approaching this level of warmth, desire, and comfort was when the Presence found me in the garden as a little girl. Any doubts about what I was doing or about Jesus being the truth, all fractured into meaningless piles of vanquished fear as I became engulfed by truth Himself. I could no longer deny He was real. I could not deny what I was experiencing.

Actually, I didn't even make it to the altar. Right there, in the middle of the aisle, too broken to wait another ten or twelve steps, my knees buckled to the floor. All the pain of living with my family—the constant abuse, the rank injustice, the absence of love, the emptiness of religion that controlled our lives without ever changing our hearts—came pouring out in a surge of awful surrender and belief.

The front of my shirt, dotted with tears, stuck to my skin as I sobbed. One of the pastors, coming over to kneel next to me, placed his hand on my shoulder and began to pray. But I couldn't hear his words or hardly acknowledge his presence. I just sat there and cried and cried and cried until I simply couldn't cry anymore.

Prior to this night, I could never imagine making such a spectacle of myself in public. I would've been too self-conscious, too concerned about what the others in the room were thinking. On this night, however, it didn't matter. Everything and everyone around me seemed to disappear in the blur of tears, prayers, and thoughts. I sat there, hugging my knees, for what seemed like ages, overwhelmed by what I had just experienced. My eyelids were shut. It all felt like a dream. Surely, I was just sitting in my bedroom. But, no, I was here. In a *Christian church*. Creating my own scandal by declaring, the only way I knew how, that I believed in Jesus Christ and that I would follow Him for the rest of my life.

Most of the congregation had quietly trickled out during the time that my little soul was rocked to its core. Soft music filled the air, mingling with the few murmurs of prayer I could still hear across the room. Taking a deep breath, looking up in exhausted relief, I caught sight of a large cross that hung in prominent view at the front of the sanctuary. I'd seen numerous crosses in my lifetime on buildings, in artwork, hanging around girls' necks. But I never really knew what it meant.

Until now.

It meant freedom. It meant hope.

It meant forgiveness, joy, and unbreakable promises.

But most of all, it meant something I never dreamed could be true.

It meant unyielding love.

A hand gently slid around my shoulder, causing me to turn sharply to see who it was. It was Angela, a warm smile radiating from her kind face. Our eyes met in a deep moment as we sat in speechless harmony. I let my head rest on her shoulder. We sat in silence for what felt like a long time. I had never felt such peace. Never.

Then, suddenly, in a shock wave of emotion, terror splashed over me. "What time is it?" I said, abruptly. But like Cinderella nearing the stroke of midnight, panic seized me without really needing an answer. I could clearly imagine my father's reaction if I were to arrive home later than nine o'clock. With sheer dread, my eyes darted across the room to the big clock that hung above the exit of the sanctuary.

All the thickness of peace I'd been feeling in this suspended hour became instantly consumed with fear. I wriggled from Angela's sweet embrace and stood to my feet.

"I have to go!" I almost shouted.

Seven

No sooner was I in the front door of my home than . . .

Rage.

Screaming.

It was everything I'd feared. And more.

"You are late! Why?! Where have you been?!"

My father's whole body was shaking with anger. His eyes bulged. His voice boomed. His jaws tightened over his clenched teeth.

Oh, how I wished I could somehow be invisible. I closed my eyes, trying to will the moment to fade, just wanting to be back in school the next day. Safe. Away from here. Anywhere.

But before I could back myself into the stairway, grasping for escape, the blur of his open hand whizzed into view and slapped hard against my cheek, raising a dark pink mark, its blunt force throwing me against the wall, as he continued screaming at me in Tamil.

"You said you were going to do homework! Were you lying to me about where you were?"

"No, Daddy, no," I said, trying my best to lie convincingly. I had no other choice. The events of that night, my disgraceful act toward him and my family's faith—all must remain a secret. There was no other way.

My mind spun with so many questions over the next few weeks and months as I tried to process what had happened to me at Angela's church. She and I shared numerous conversations, some in the lunchroom, some over the phone. Whenever we talked by phone, we'd use code words for certain terms—like "the letter" instead of the Bible—in order to maintain secrecy. But for every answer she gave me, a new question rushed to take its place.

The thing I struggled the most to understand was who Jesus was. Islam had taught me that Jesus was a prophet, like Abraham and Moses were prophets. He wasn't God; He was just a man. And even Christians say, yes, He was a man who lived here on earth. So how could a man be born of God? How could a man *be* God? Yet to be a Christian, I was expected to worship Him? To worship a man? A man who died on a cross? It was all confusing and contradictory to everything I'd been taught.

Yet whenever my perplexing thoughts frustrated me, I would close my eyes and instantly be transported back to memories of that night, that moment, that sweet woman's praise in the seat near me, that riveting experience of my own with God. I could not deny the power of it all, the unforgettable sense of belonging and assurance when my world suddenly stopped and He touched me with His presence. What I'd experienced that night was more real than life itself.

Although I couldn't go to church on Sundays without risking unwanted notice, I did find ways to get back into the church building and reflect on what happened, to ponder God and worship Him in a place that had become incredibly special to me. One day Angela said she was involved in a meeting at church, scheduled for an upcoming weeknight. Would I like to come along, she asked, just to pray alone in the sanctuary?

Her invitation shot chills of terror through me, knowing it would require making up another story for my parents. Could I risk it all again? I didn't know. And yet, at the same time, how could I not? The question didn't even need to be asked. I was all in. Since I craved to touch God again like before, deceiving my parents felt somewhat justifiable despite my pangs of guilt.

Not too many days later, I found myself in the same sanctuary, standing before the same wooden cross, feeling the same rush of emotion and conviction I'd experienced a few months prior. No music this night, of course. Just a handful of teenage voices in the distance, their laughter and conversation carrying through the building. The only Presence that mattered to me was the one drawing me even closer to my newfound faith. He was coaxing me toward Him, making me want to be engulfed by Him.

I wept loud heaves of tears as I knelt before the cross alone, declaring my love and allegiance to Him, wanting to be changed by Him, asking Him to give me boldness and grace to love my difficult family.

Belief was taking hold.

But, still, so much was at stake.

Even with Angela talking to me and encouraging me day after day, how could I ever know what I was supposed to do next? Waterfalls of tears and hidden desire could only take me so far, only tell me so much. Where was this path really leading me? Was I strong enough to survive what it could easily cost?

A few weeks later Angela said with eager excitement, "I have something for you!" She slipped her backpack onto the desk, telling me to close my eyes while she unzipped it.

Smiling, I wondered what this gift could possibly be. I could hear her rummaging through her bag as I impatiently swayed back and forth, waiting, feeling so thankful for this sweet friend I was growing to love, who was always surprising me with her tenderness and devotion.

"Okay, open your eyes!" she finally said in a singsong voice.

Looking into her cupped hands, I saw something like a small journal. Grayish blue and adorned with a small, dainty medallion.

"It's a Bible," she said, folding back the cover to reveal the writing inside.

A Bible? Of my very own?

At first, not yet realizing the full significance of the Bible and how imperatively I needed one, I was mostly struck with what it meant to be receiving this from Angela. Not only had she gone to all the effort and thoughtfulness to give me a present, but I could tell from the look of love

and affection on her face that she was sharing with me the most precious
thing she could give.

I snatched it from her hands and flipped through the delicate pages.
My own Bible! A friend had loaned me one that I'd kept stashed in the
back corner of my locker. But to have one that actually belonged to me! It
left me speechless.

I impulsively hugged her tight, letting her know she couldn't have
given me a more perfect gift.

"It's small so you can hide it," she whispered, a wink of knowledge
that touched me at a deep place in my heart. Because, yes, as lovely and
intriguing as this copy of the Bible would be to me, it would also be an
incriminating piece of evidence. I knew that. So did she. How meaningful
that she would think of such a specific, personal detail, making sure it
didn't have a title on the cover or spine or anywhere.

My own Bible.

And my own friend.

I needed both of them more than anyone could know.

Hiding my blossoming faith wasn't as easy as concealing my Bible. I would
stay up late to pray and silently worship while my parents slept. Even when
they were awake, I would often read my Bible in the bathroom, where they
couldn't see. As often as possible, I would sneak out to attend prayer meetings and other functions at Angela's church. Each new venture and getaway upped my risk of being found out, of course, but my growing love for
Jesus led me to become increasingly daring. The deception still bothered
my conscience—more and more all the time—but the reward of getting
to know Him was becoming worth the risk.

The Bible, though terribly confusing at first, in terms of how it's arranged and where I was supposed to start reading, proved to be a treasure
of truth and life to me. It was my secret companion. Some nights, like

when reading Jesus's parables in the Gospels, I would grasp my hair in frustration, wanting so badly to understand what He meant, yet feeling hopelessly lost in the translation. But on other nights, the presence of God would illuminate a verse or teaching with such blow-me-away clarity, I would cry a grateful prayer for how personally and powerfully He was revealing Himself to me.

The family tension at home, however, continued growing as well. The light inside my spirit that was more frequently bringing a smile to my face wasn't being reflected at all in my circumstances. One night, in fact, as I was feeling a little more full of joyful energy than I usually showed at home, my father lunged out of nowhere and struck me in the chest with a crushing blow. I fell to the floor, shaken.

That's what was becoming so freakishly infuriating about the whole thing: how unpredictably his anger could spark. I could be doing nothing. *Nothing,* it seemed. And then—bang!—his brutal gaze, his threatening voice, more random acts of violence.

Gathering my balance and running to my room for hopeful safety, I yearned to yell back, "I loathe you!" with every decibel of breath I could muster. But all I could do, all I could ever do, was try to put walls and doors between me and his erratic rage. Retaliation was unthinkable. Being weak and defenseless—which were the necessary ingredients for his wrathful forms of abuse—was the only option available to me.

But not on this night.

As soon as I got to my room and pushed the door shut behind me, I yanked the covers off my bed to unveil the secret that hid beneath. Frantically tossing pages back and forth, I wondered where they kept the parts that could speak to my soul in that moment and soothe the agony I felt. Finally settling on page one as the place to start, I began reading to myself in a seething whisper, "In the beginning God created the heavens and the earth."

And almost instantly the anger in my heart that ached for revenge turned into a place for God's divine comfort to be housed. These words of power, glory, and beauty settled around me for the very first time.

"The earth was without form, and void; and darkness was on the face of the deep. And the Spirit of God was hovering over the face of the waters."

There He was.

From the very beginning of time, all the way to this date on the calendar, right there in the modest Ohio neighborhood where a little Muslim girl quaked under her father's abuse and longed for answers that she wanted to believe were out there, God was already working His wonders. Fashioning the heavens and the earth. Moving among the formless darkness of an uncreated universe.

He was here.

He was everything I'd been searching for.

If I didn't know before, He was assuring me now.

Suddenly, I was traveling back in time to a scene from my childhood, the scenic view of a Sri Lankan sunset displayed across the canvas of my memory. The sky had seemed so immeasurably big to my little-girl eyes that late afternoon, and I vividly remember wondering to myself who had painted it so beautifully.

Equally enormous questions had continued to follow me throughout my young but difficult life, questions concerning my own worth and existence: Why am I here? Why do my lungs breathe? Why does my heart beat? And every time I'd encountered a crossroads that caused these types of questions to register with me again, I'd never been able to find a suitable answer to satisfy what my inquisitive mind wished to know. Despite the hours I'd invested into being the best Muslim I could be, Islam didn't seem capable of dealing with what my heart wanted—no, *needed*—to know.

And yet here, in this fascinating retelling of creation, in the face of God's desire for friendship with humanity, all of it made perfect sense.

I existed for *Him,* the One who made me.

He knew who I was, and He was allowing me to know Him.

And the more I immersed myself in reading the Bible, the more convinced I became that this truth was what I'd been searching my whole life to discover.

On my warm bed that night I felt His hope and healing unfolding within me.

In the journey of my salvation, I was inching deeper and deeper into the ocean of God's unconditional love and truth. I was slowly moving away from the roots of Islam, tradition, and honor, moving passionately, head-on toward a mysterious Presence named Jesus Christ. And by His grace, this mystery was beginning to resolve in slow, simple bites that He knew I was ready to receive.

In the beginning, He had made the heavens and the earth.

And in the meantime, this truth was enough for me.

Eight

❖

In the spring, around six months after that momentous first night of prayer, faith, and worship at Angela's church, she invited me to a weekend youth retreat, wondering if we could somehow pull it off. Putting our heads together, we figured out a way to convince my parents that it was a school-sponsored event focused on improving our writing skills. I was torn with guilt by the fact that I was lying again. How was I honoring God or my parents by doing this? Yet the desire in my heart to worship Jesus overpowered even my remorse in lying to my parents, and I moved forward in executing our plan. I hoped that God would understand my situation.

Nonetheless, they bought it.

So we were lying there in our cabins, the last night of the weekend, and I turned to her and said, "So, Angela . . ."

With a smirk, she cut her eyes playfully toward me. "Let me guess. Another question." She and I had become so close since that incredible night of the past September and through our many experiences together since then that she'd started anticipating whenever I was coming at her with another string of relentless questions about Christianity. We both laughed at how predictable I was.

"Yes. So tell me again, what are all the rules I'm supposed to follow?"

"Like I told you," she said, patiently as always, "there aren't any."

"None?"

"Right. None."

"Really? You're sure about that?"

"When you're a Christian," she told me, "you obey God because you want to, because He's changing you, because He's made you a new person on the inside. It's not like you just go out and sin as much as you like and don't worry about it. But at the same time, you don't need to do anything to make God love you."

I contemplated the freedom implied in this logic. "You mean, like, I can eat whatever I want?"

"Yeah. Sure."

Because in my Muslim upbringing, we were forbidden from eating any meat that's not *halal,* meaning it's not a permissible type of meat, or the animal is cut in a forbidden way, or without invoking the name of Allah while cutting and preparing the permissible meat. Ordering or trying a bite of meat in any non-halal restaurant, for example, could've been considered a sin for me by my Muslim family. My family took very seriously this matter of eating halal meat, exclusively. I assumed Christianity would require something similar.

This kind of eye-opening discovery was becoming commonplace as I grew in my new faith, because the differences between Christianity and Islam were astonishingly extreme. Islam, for example, requires many outward sacrifices and actions. It means praying five times a day. It means restraining from certain types of food and dress. Some extremist Muslims may sanction violence for the sake of retaining Islamic honor. In many ways, Islam is a list of (mostly) don'ts sprinkled with a few significant dos. And if not followed precisely and properly, it means shame and oppression for the unfaithful.

Christianity, however (I was finding out), is much more than rules and religious obligations or even honor. It revolves around our internal nature, our heart, which in many ways is an even *greater* sacrifice than mere adherence to codes of conduct and disciplined achievement. It's about a personal relationship with God Himself. It's about love. In Matthew 22, for instance, a lawyer asked Jesus, "Teacher, which is the greatest commandment in the law?" to which He responded, "You shall love the

LORD your God with all your heart, with all your soul, and with all your mind" (verses 36–37).

And for the purposes of my question to Angela, I learned that Christianity is certainly not hung up on what kinds of food to eat or not eat. Like the Bible says in Romans 14:17, "For the kingdom of God is not eating and drinking, but righteousness and peace and joy in the Holy Spirit."

So the next school day, after we got back from our weekend trip, I could hardly contain myself as I stood in line at the cafeteria. My parents weren't there to watch me as I took the plate from our school chef and sat down at a nearby table. The aroma rising up from my choice of entrée was enough to make my starving belly rumble even more. I was giddy. I could hardly wait for my first taste.

What an indescribable thrill of liberty I felt, biting into my first-ever slice of pepperoni pizza. I polished off the entire thing without feeling a shred of guilt.

I can't believe it, I thought to myself in awe. *I can eat whatever I want.*

Although Christianity was measurably freeing to a new convert, I was also getting my first taste of why it also involves an even greater sacrifice than Islam. I was discovering, in taking the Bible and Angela's answers to their logical conclusions, that devotion to Christ meant giving Him *everything:* my time, my energy, my thoughts, my resources, my dreams. It meant denying myself and willfully allowing His new life to transform my heart from the inside out.

Take my family's anger and abuse toward me, for example. This new faith of mine required that I restrain from boiling with anger toward them or in desiring to take revenge against them for hurting me. Rather, I was supposed to pray for them, forgive them, and love them as Christ loved His enemies. It didn't mean being a doormat, not defending myself, but it did mean my response toward them, because of Christ's new life in me, could actually be characterized by the genuine strength of God's love instead of the selfish, artificial strength of anger.

This was all so different than what I'd learned in Islam, but I was determined to go all in. I was ready to become a "perfect" Christian overnight.

But despite my high level of desire and enthusiasm, I learned (and am still learning), this part of Christianity is a prolonged process. True, my life was no longer my own. I belonged to Jesus, and He was now in charge of me. But yielding myself to Him in all these areas where I'd always reacted on sheer impulse before . . .

Let's just say it was taking time.

I would still cuss. I would still gossip about people. I would still get mad and fume or get selfish and pout. Sometimes, in some of my lowest, most frustrating moments, I worried that *nothing* had really changed.

During the early part of my freshman year, for example, still struggling with a hunger for approval, I had boldly tried out for the cheerleading squad, thinking it would help me fit in. I knew, of course, my parents would never tolerate such a thing. Short skirts? Dance formations? Boys watching me from the sidelines? As immigrants, my parents didn't really know what cheerleading even was. I masked my involvement by using the excuse of a school project or special assignment that required the extra time. Because I knew they wouldn't approve of the cheerleading outfit, I would leave the house in sweatpants or my regular clothes, not changing or putting on my uniform until I'd reached the place we were going.

But fairly soon after I had given this a try, God showed me very plainly that my desperation for acceptance was a fool's errand. From mean girls to leering boys, the whole experience left me feeling more misunderstood than ever. I saw and felt how unfulfilling the allure of popularity always ends up being. God's presence was what I really wanted and needed, not the fake, fragile mirage of others' approval.

Yet as I continued to struggle with my actions and reactions, deep down I knew something was different about me from the person I'd been before. Even though I was often still provoked to anger by my father or my family, even though I could still harbor certain thoughts and attitudes that obviously needed to be replaced with better ones, I was beginning to sense—for the first time in my life—a new kind of peace in my heart and deep compassion for people that sometimes overwhelmed me in the most precious way. For the first time in my life, I felt I could truly see through God's eyes and feel what He felt. I could see the homeless and feel the sting of reproach in which they lived their lives. I could see my brother striving for acceptance and love from my father and feeling the pain of his constant rejection. I could see the popular girls at school and feel their emptiness and desire to have more than outward beauty. I could see creation—the flowers, the birds in the air, the smell of the morning dew—and feel the joy of my Father in heaven delighting in His creation. This compassion was definitely something I had never experienced before until my commitment to follow Christ.

However, some days I wondered if any change had occurred at all.

My big brother, for instance, could still get under my skin. He would say such mean things to me, and I'd want to give them right back to him, even meaner. I remember hauling a load of heavy grocery bags into the house one day, all by myself, while he sat there too engrossed in his video game to help me. When I walked by for the last time, cutting him a hostile look, he sort of glanced my direction, kept pounding on his game controls, and said, "What's up, one-eyed b—h?"

"Shut up!" I snapped, seething with anger, then ran to my room and cried, not so much hurt by what he said but by the harsh way I'd chosen to respond. Why couldn't I react to him with love the way Jesus would have?

Like I said, it was a slow process.

But then, at other times, I would be consumed with growing my affection for him and wanting him to somehow experience Christ through my actions. One year, for his birthday, for instance, I became obsessed with finding the perfect gift. Birthdays in our family were not that big a deal. In all my years of growing up, I don't recall once being celebrated on my birthday or showered with gifts, not that my parents were being cruel. Where I come from, people don't go party crazy over birthdays the way they do in America. I'd never given (nor had I ever been *expected* to give) a present to my brother on his birthday.

I decided, though, as a pure act of kindness, I was ready to change that.

I pondered this puzzle and prayed about it for weeks, trying to think of what I could possibly give him that would meet a need and make an impact. Finally I landed on the idea of wide receiver gloves. He'd recently started playing football, and he'd been borrowing a pair from someone. I didn't know what made these gloves such an essential part of his athletic gear, but I knew they were very important to him, and I knew he didn't have any. What if I saved my money and bought him a pair of his own? It would be more than just a piece of equipment. Maybe it would be the start of a new relationship.

It would be perfect.

"Oh, here," I said, when the big day arrived, sort of awkwardly tossing the gloves wrapped in pretty paper at him and mumbling a faint "happy birthday," then walking off to my room, dancing with joy at what I'd done. I couldn't believe it. Did I really just give him a birthday gift?

It might not sound like a big deal to you, but the love I felt for my brother in that moment, a love that had been growing each day as I thought about what I wanted to give him, as I went to the store to pick out the gift, as I prayed about what his reaction would be and what this simple gesture might touch off in him . . .

It was transformational.

The only thing that could top it, I believe, was the next time *my* birthday approached. One afternoon as I walked around with him at a local shopping place, he pointed to a bright pink dress and said, "Rifqa, what do you think of this color?"

That's how I found myself holding that same dress in my trembling hands a few weeks later on my birthday.

Unexpected. Unbelievable.

Maybe the Lord really *was* up to something.

Ups and downs. Highs and lows. These were seasons of real progress as well as moments when God painfully made clear to me again why popularity doesn't satisfy, why others' love doesn't satisfy, why money and the things it can buy don't satisfy, why fantasizing about a different set of circumstances doesn't satisfy. Why *nothing* else satisfies except Jesus and whatever I allow Him to transform in my life to reflect His loving touch on my soul.

And little by little, He was making a new Rifqa out of me.

I had managed to keep my new faith a secret for a whole year. Not by taking it casually, but by taking it underground. Then one afternoon the next fall, I got my first definable heads-up about two very important things. First, I wouldn't be able to hide forever. Second, God would always be there to protect me.

I was sitting in my bedroom, finishing my homework for the day. Sunlight gleamed through the window as I was penciling and erasing a frustratingly difficult math problem. I can still see the calculator resting in my hand, can still remember every detail of the precise moment when this strange but strong internal nudge—barely a whisper in my mind— somehow warned me to take my Bible out of my backpack and hide it.

I had been growing more and more familiar with this gentle whisper, and I was trying to be better about heeding its timely wisdom. So I acted on it quickly and without questioning. I shoved my Bible underneath a pile of clothes in my messy closet. "There," I said, as I slid the closet door shut.

Later on that evening, I had my backpack lying close to the dining room table. My father, unannounced and saying nothing, picked up my backpack and started rummaging through it, feeling in all the corners, digging and tugging. Obviously on a mission. Trying as hard as I could to hide my taut emotions, I asked him, "Do you need something?"

"I was looking for a pencil," he said, finally pulling a pink mechanical one from the bowels of the backpack before letting it slide to the floor.

I breathed a heart-racing sigh of relief and tried to assume the appearance of total tranquility as I raced to my bedroom. I couldn't help but release an inaudible scream. I jumped up and down, mouthing the words, "Oh my word! *Oh my word!* OH! MY! WORD!"

Nine

R ifqa! Why are you not praying?"
My mother's voice echoed louder as she approached my room.
Groaning inwardly, I got up from my bed.

"It is time for selah," she said, entering to see what I was doing. "And look at you. You are not even moving to get washed for prayer. What has happened to you?"

She was wearing peach-colored prayer garments that covered her entire body, and she carried a white prayer outfit for me, along with a green prayer mat, both of which she threw at me in exasperation.

"Go! Pray!" she ordered, scowling as I passed her.

Exchanges like these were becoming more common in my house. She and my father had not overlooked the obvious decline in my dedication to Islam. They saw how I'd gritted my teeth at each call to prayer. They picked up on the silence coming from my room—silence that was supposed to be filled with recitations from the Qur'an. The gap between me and my family's Islamic culture was visibly widening.

A few months later, several members of our Islamic community were gathered in our home during the customary weekly meeting, where a few families get together to worship and hear their children recite the Qur'an. The room was fragrant with the candles we burned for prayer. I watched the smoke rising to the ceiling, wishing that I, too, could trail away and find something else to do. I didn't want to be there, and I'm sure my face silently screamed it. Was I compromising my Christian faith by participating in this, even though I didn't mean a word of it? That's all I could seem to think about. But I knew I needed to push all these thoughts aside as my turn came around to recite the verses, delivering the prescribed excerpt in a lifeless, monotone voice: "LAAAA-illaaha-illullaaaah . . ."

I looked over at my mother's pained expression; she looked embarrassed by my lack of wholeheartedness. My father bore his eyes into mine as well, as if to direct me to speak louder and put more energy into it. Out of fear of him, I pepped it up with a little more gusto.

Later on that evening, after the guests had left, my mother approached me. "What is this nonsense, Rifqa? Did you hear Nadia? How far she is in memorizing the Qur'an? You are a disgrace! Why can't you be more like her?"

The tension kept escalating. And it was sure to *keep* escalating.

It didn't help matters to know summer was slowly approaching, which for most kids at school meant the glorious end of a nine-month jail sentence. The atmosphere in the school hallway was spinning with excitement as students chatted about their summer plans, barely able to contain the excitement of their impending freedom.

"I can't wait to lay out at the pool and get a tan this summer. Bikinis, here we come!"

"Hey, dude, you gonna come with us? We're grabbing some dinner and going to see a movie tonight."

I'd hear it all, I'd sense it all, but my only choice was to walk away from it all—not that I wanted to go mindlessly chill with most of them anyway. If given my preference, I'd want to go to church and sing my head off in worship, imagining a life where everyone—my parents included—would be inspired and overjoyed by my zeal for following Christ. No, the reason why end-of-school landed with such a thud in my heart was because for me, a young female teenager in a strict Muslim family, summertime was the epitome of misery.

I wasn't allowed to go anywhere other than the mosque, and I could see no one other than my immediate family. Walking out the door to hang out with my friends was forbidden. My mother would say things like, "Did you know, Rifqa, that when I was your age, I never went out of the house until it was past six o'clock? That was so men would not see me and I would not tempt them." Picturing her in a hijab and burka, I couldn't help but sarcastically think, *How alluring.*

Summer also meant extra hours of Islamic classes, which made regular school seem like a thrill ride at a theme park. It was also my parents' prescription for fixing what was wrong in my religious devotion.

"It is an honor to worship Allah, Rifqa, and you are disgracing us," my mother said. "The worst decision we made was bringing you to America. We want you to have a strong foundation like we did when we grew up in Sri Lanka. That's why we are putting you in more Islamic classes."

More Islamic classes. Ugh.

So without any strength or right to oppose, I went to the daily six-hour classes when summer began. Each long, miserably hot day was filled with reciting passages from the Qur'an in Arabic for hours at a time and learning about the history of Islamic faith. I was sure the drudgery would've been bad enough, even if I wasn't completely turned off by the subject matter I was being forced to hear. But sitting there, trying to hold in the tension between my two conflicting worlds, was almost unbearable. All the doctrines I was being taught, all the exercises I was participating in, went totally against everything I now believed in. I realized my only option was no option at all: putting everything on the line, offering life and limb to declare my allegiance to Jesus. But being force-fed Islamic instruction when all I wanted was to learn more about Christ and the Bible was a rare form of torture.

After about the third week of summer classes, staring blankly one day at the woman who was leading us, a rebellious idea came to me, triggering a smile that tugged at the corner of my lips. Her black hijab tightened around her face as she taught in front of the classroom. Her expression was stern and unappealing. But feeling this devious plan conspiring inside me, I perked up in fake interest while reaching innocently into my bag to pull out a notebook.

Only it wasn't just a notebook; it was the beloved journal I'd been using to catalog the runaway thoughts I could tell no one besides God and myself. Writing in my journal, although inviting danger if these personal scribblings were ever found and exposed to the light, had become my escape. I would spend hours writing letters to God, pouring out my heart, journaling my fears and frustrations, my dreams and passions. I don't know how I could've made it across the high wire of those anxious months if I hadn't been able to put my prayers and heartfelt appeals down on paper. Writing it out resulted in a backflow of comfort I'd never felt at any other time in my life.

On this day, though, I spotted an opening for journaling time that I'd never considered before. Pretending to be taking notes from our teacher's lecture, I daringly drove my pen in another direction.

June 9

Lord, I am here in a Muslim prayer session, praying to you, O God. I don't believe in what they are teaching me. Lord, I pray that you would help me block out everything they are saying. I know you put me in here for a reason. Sitting here and being forced to listen to what's been bringing me so much pain is just . . . misery . . . although it's not going to stop me from worshiping you. Nothing will. I am going to stay here for you, O Sovereign Lord.

It's like every day I am here, they talk about how wrong Christians are. Have they ever thought they could be the ones that are wrong? I have a lot of

*bitterness and hatred inside me. I pray that you will
take the bitterness away and fill me with your love, to
even love these girls here in the Islamic Center. I have
so much anger inside me for being forced to come. I
pray that you take it all away.*

    Amen.

Emboldened by my treachery, I committed an even greater transgression the next day. We were required to wear a hijab and a traditional Islamic dress called a *kurtah* to our classes at the mosque. But that morning, as I was getting ready, I conceived a way to work this wardrobe to my advantage, sticking my iPod through the long kurtah and letting the ear buds hang at the side of my face. To my delight, the dark hijab completely covered them. I looked in the bathroom mirror thrilled and scared at the same time as I covered my dark hair with the hijab.

At one point during class, I reached underneath my hijab, pretending to fix it, and hastily plunged the headphones into my ears. Quiet worship music immediately flooded into my soul, even while the Qur'an was being read and recited around me.

Creatively integrating Christian faith into my Muslim life became a sport to me. I recall walking with the impatient rush of women into our mosque one day, nearly being knocked over by their haste to squeeze through its little door. Once inside, yellow light illuminated the room as I took off my sandals and assumed my position of prayer. To my left and right, fully covered women were neatly lined up like dominoes while a powerful masculine voice broke the eerie silence, chanting, "Alllllaaaaaahu Akbar Alllllaaaaaahu Akbar." Each of us, like robots, dropped rhythmically to the floor, performing our stipulated observance.

But though my body was knelt prostrate to Allah, my heart was bowing before my new Lord and King. And underneath the echoed din of "Subash-haduanna Muhhammadan-Rasulullah," I whispered my own version of daily prayer, saying, "Lord, I worship You. You are the one true living God. Jesus, I bow to You and no other name."

I wondered if I was the first to ever speak His name in worship within these rustic walls.

I also wondered how much longer I could lead this double life.

Ten

My parents' concern understandably increased as the new school year started, even though I don't think their suspicions had ever formalized toward the actual truth. A few times they discovered Christian books or materials in my room, but I'd been able to brush it all away as simply "working on a school research project." Except for snippets of conversations they might have overheard from school friends, either mentioning my Bible or making fun of my faith, I was seeming to succeed at keeping my mother and father marginally in the dark. Not that I found any sly satisfaction in that part, but it was my only means of staying within the circle of other Christians. Being honest with my parents about my whereabouts at all times was simply not a livable option, in terms of going to a random Bible study or a special event.

We moved from our rental house to an apartment, and some of the natural distractions of packing and unpacking and resettling into a new place occupied a lot of everyone's attention, making my freedom of movement a little bit easier. Plus when my father was traveling (which was most of the time), my mother gave me so little attention that my excuses generally sufficed, if they weren't bunched too frequently together. I even took a part-time job as a waitress at a small restaurant—another outing I occasionally used as a reason for needing to leave the house during non-school hours. I was desperate to be released from the controlling grip of Islam and be embraced by the comfort of my brothers and sisters in Christ or to simply be out of my stifling home life. Yet the hardest part was the route to get there—lying. The gritting of teeth. Making up a fake story. It never got easy. Although it was the only way to survive emotionally, my heart always felt the pang that this was wrong. It was a painful, guilt-inducing way to live.

The uptick in my Christian activities was inevitably leading me toward being discovered. I knew it. And though I was aware of the growing risk each time I stepped up my public visibility—each time I snuck out of the house or came home from school later than usual—the intoxication of being with other Christians and participating in prayer meetings and other church functions was just too exciting for me to forsake. Jesus had so inspired my heart to follow Him that I was willing to become increasingly daring. I was daily becoming more blind to the very real consequences of what I was doing as I fell deeper and deeper in love with Him.

Being back in school was helpful after my horrible summer. Being able to interact with other kids outside my family's tight circle of connections within Islam provided a blessed breath of relief. The only real bummer of the new term was that Angela was gone. She had moved to another school district. I missed her terribly. We spoke by phone often for a little while, but as the weeks passed our calls became less and less frequent. I was left to make other friends inside the church and Christian community. And thankfully, though with much trepidation, I slowly began to cross paths with them.

One way that I met new people was through my secretive participation in youth group at church that was going to perform an interpretive dance for an event. I had been practicing for months, though because I couldn't let my parents know about this, I actually did most of my practicing by twirling alone in my bedroom while watching a YouTube video the leader had prepared especially for me. We were gearing up to present our number at a café night of artistic worship at the church, and I was on pins and needles, knowing this event would put me on stage in front of way more people than I had any business alerting to my presence.

Actually, it even got a little worse than that. Our dance leader, despite my timid wincing and objections, insisted that I appear at the front of the group to open our routine. So we did our thing, flowed together as best we could, and hoped the audience was moved to worship by what they saw and felt.

The music ended, and shouts of applause showered from every corner of the room. My father, of course, wasn't there to see me, but I had never felt the love of my heavenly Father more genuinely than in that exhilarating moment.

"You all looked like angels dancing," the pastor said after we completed our set, causing my cheeks to redden in embarrassment. When the event finally broke up for the night, a woman I'd never met approached me and said, "Hey, my name is Shaniqua. You did an amazing job!"

"Thank you."

"How old are you?" she asked.

"Fourteen."

She interestedly kept asking questions about who I was and where I was from until we finally exchanged phone numbers and hoped to continue our conversation later. "But just so you know," I said, "if I call you, I have to be very careful. I can't say anything that relates to Christianity because my parents are Muslim."

Her relaxed demeanor became instantly tense.

"Oh, really?"

"Yeah."

"Well," she said, after a momentary pause, as if giving herself permission to say it, "I'd still love to stay in touch with you, Rifqa."

"I'd love that as well."

Shaniqua was about ten years older than I, and she became like a big sister and mentor to me. We rarely saw each other, out of pains for our protection. But our many late-night phone calls—several a week, often at two or three in the morning—were lifelines of hope and encouragement to my heart. I lived for those moments more than I lived for sleep. After those conversations I was desperate to give myself to Christ in a deeper way. She came to understand my situation, and I knew I could reach out to her if I ever needed help.

Through Shaniqua, I met another girl, Michaela, not quite as old as Shaniqua but still a big sister's difference in age to me. I'd been sharing with Shaniqua in some of our phone calls how burdened I felt for the kids in my school, how almost none of them seemed to know Jesus, and how even the ones who claimed to be Christians didn't live as though He made any difference to them at all.

"You know who you sound like? A girl I know named Michaela, who's a student now at Ohio State. What I hear in your heart reminds me so much of her. I really think you two would enjoy connecting."

So that's how I found myself at a Starbucks across the street from my high school with a new Christian friend whose gray eyes seemed to glisten with grace and love. I don't remember exactly what Michaela and I talked about, but I do remember walking with her to the car afterward, and how she continued sitting there with me, listening to me share my story and the heaviness of my heart. Unable to harness my emotions, my voice finally broke into sobs over the real pain I felt for my unsaved friends at school as well as the pain of living in my home and trying to maintain the juggling act my days had become. She tenderly rubbed my back as the sunset painted her windshield in purple and orange shades of autumn beauty.

Like with Shaniqua, I never did spend a lot of face-to-face time with Michaela, although each time I had the privilege, she bolstered my faith with the open authenticity of her own. Her advice and involvement contributed tremendously to how I viewed life, counseling me on how to disengage from relationships in high school that weren't strengthening my faith while still caring for those same people with the deep love of Christ.

Then she introduced me to another friend, who would become perhaps the most influential of all: Brian.

Brian was in charge of a prayer meeting held every Saturday outside an abortion clinic in Columbus. Everyone spoke of him in such glowing terms, and to me, the idea of standing with other believers and praying for (perhaps praying with) women who were considering putting an end to their pregnancies fired me with excitement. I hadn't been able to go to church in months because of increased scrutiny at home, and this seed of a ministry opportunity intrigued me enough to follow it up. I was able to find Brian on Facebook, begin a conversation, and then arrange a way with Shaniqua for someone to drive me there.

Brian is a big teddy bear of a guy who, when he talks about Jesus (which is most of the time), makes you want to drop whatever you're doing and go find somebody, anybody, who's hurting without the Lord. He has firsthand stories of leading the homeless and drug addicts to Christ out on the streets. He lives and breathes Jesus with every moment. If I needed any more convincing that the rest of my life would be promised wholeheartedly to God—no matter how close to the grave it took me—Brian's spiritual passion sent me flying off the cliff of my final doubt. Whenever I was within his inspiring orbit or getting to know some of the other Ohio State University kids who hung out with him and lived out a wholehearted faith, I knew exactly where my ultimate loyalties were meant to lie.

"Is that little Rifqa?" he'd say whenever I spun into view at any gathering where the two of us were around. I'd run with all my strength and be swallowed up by his big embrace. Most of the other men in my life—my dad, my uncle, my big brother—used their power and position to abuse, dictate, and manipulate. Brian was the first one I ever felt safe with, somebody who respected and protected me and basically fathered me like one of his spiritual children.

"I don't ever want you to get hurt by anyone," he'd say. "Especially one of those little skinny-jeaned skater boys with only one thing on their mind. I'm on the watch for you, Rifqa, and I'm willing to hurt somebody if they ever do anything to you."

Though he couldn't completely relate with what my home life and family were all about—who could?—Brian understood me enough to encourage and cheerlead. "Remember, Rifqa, what you're going through is not pointless. God is shaping you into a mighty woman of God, and sometimes that means taking people through some very difficult circumstances that shape and mold them into someone special. It's a beautiful story He's writing in you. And He's fighting for you. Don't you ever give up," he'd say, peering into my scared caramel eyes.

But sometimes that's all I felt like doing.

Giving up.

The constant secrecy and turmoil, mixed with fear and panic at being found out, was more than my heart could always hold inside. And as another school year drew to a close—realizing my window of access to others was about to be sealed off for another summer—I sat next to my friend Katie one day and toyed with telling her some of what was going on at home.

Katie and I had been close friends in eighth grade. She had even come over to my house once; she was one of the few who ever had. The fact that she was African American, I think, made my parents more open to inviting her in. As a result, she had more of an inkling than anybody else for how strict my family was. She'd seen it up close.

Katie and I had lost track of each other as freshmen because we didn't have any classes together that year, but we had reconnected as sophomores. In fact, a few weeks earlier, she had nudged me after I'd finished a physics assignment and said, "Wow, Rifqa, I can't believe you're reading your Bible in class." She wasn't making fun of me. I think she was commenting on the social pressures we can all feel so bound by, and how refreshed it made her feel to see somebody who didn't seem to care. The truth was, I *did* care, too much actually, and I hated whenever I felt myself caving in to it. Yet my love for Christ overflowed like a well, and the hunger to know Him was so strong, it often helped me stay above the pettiness of peer pressure.

That's about when she and I started sitting next to each other on the daily bus ride to and from school. Her brother had graduated the previous year and could no longer drive her. And even though we didn't hang out during the day in the same social groups, our friendship revived during those times together in the bus. She became again the special friend I had known her to be in years past.

"Katie?" I said, taking a chance she'd listen as we bumped along on our way home. She seemed to notice right off that something was serious in my tone of voice. "I have something to tell you," and I told her everything. Or at least everything I thought she could handle without thinking I was crazy or paranoid. She'd witnessed enough of my family's behavior to believe me when I said I was in deep trouble. I prayed she'd hear me out.

"I just don't know what to do," I said as I hurried to wrap things up before reaching the bus stop. Concern radiated from her face, and she touched my arm to comfort me when she saw the fear in my eyes. She didn't judge me; she simply listened. That's all I really wanted.

"Rifqa, you know you're more than welcome to stay with me and my family if you ever need to," she said with compassion.

How nice of her. I hoped she knew how much her gesture meant to me, but I could never take her up on her offer. Wherever I went, my father would find me. I couldn't put anybody else in the path of his fury.

Yet with the passing of time, God was positioning people in my life who proved instrumental in shepherding me through my unique challenges and choices of faith, uphill battles that I could never have kept ascending alone. I still had no way to clearly predict what the coming days would entail, but He was providing me with some flesh-and-blood backup, just in case.

Just in case.

I filled in the last blank on my last exam and turned in my paper to the Spanish teacher. School was now officially over for me for the year. I was done.

Exiting the classroom, I was delighted to find the hallway completely empty. My footsteps echoed on the polished floor and clicked in staccato against the ceiling and walls. I looked down to adore the bright pink dress my brother had given me as I slowly twirled. My home life, of course, combined with the new summer's confinement, loomed over me with foreboding. Yet I reveled in the satisfaction that I was in the Lord's hands and would get through the next few months somehow.

I dragged my fingers across each locker as I walked, a small tradition I'd acquired by walking through the hallway and praying for my classmates. Nearly every locker I touched belonged to an unknown face and name, and I'd often brought them in bulk to the Father, asking for His blessing. Today was no different, although as I reached the place where the bank of lockers ended, I verbalized a prayer and promise for myself as well: "Even though I walk through the valley of the shadow of death, I will not fear . . . for You are with me."

As I stepped outside into the warm sun, an inaudible voice seemed to whisper a reply that nearly frightened me at first, yet sparked me with a sudden excitement. *You're not coming back here, Rifqa.* I seemed to know it. This was the end. This summer would represent for me the burning of some bridges and the paving of some new roads.

I turned to gaze again at the gargantuan white columns that fronted those familiar maroon walls, standing like a skyscraper above my small stature, the words *New Albany* inscribed in regal grace across the top of the building. I had stood here and witnessed this sight every school day, ever since we'd moved to this state. I was standing there at that moment, squinting into the sun and clutching the straps of my backpack. And something told me I would never stand here again.

Eleven

Although I had completely given my heart to Christ by the time I turned sixteen, there was one act of complete abandonment that I still desired.

I wanted to be baptized.

The church where I'd been mostly involved—Angela's—was leery about doing this for me. When I say I was involved there, of course, I don't mean like being a faithful attendee. My home life obviously didn't allow for regular, unexplainable absences between nine o'clock and noon on a Sunday morning. But I went whenever I could, and I was involved in other ways around whatever periphery I could afford to mask. Still, while they accepted me and showed me Jesus in such sweet, personal ways, they didn't quite know how to handle a lone sheep whose presence in their flock might attract some serious wolves. They worried, I believe, that any official affiliation with their church on my part could expose them to the kind of legal and public-perception tangles that get churches on the front page of newspapers. So their suggestion to me—which might have been informed by wisdom but was probably more informed by fear—was to let them minister to me despite my unusual situation but not to think about baptism until I was eighteen.

I didn't think I could wait that long.

But unlike most sixteen-year-olds wishing to declare their devotion to Christ—and sadly, much like everything else that happened in my life—this would not be an easy thing to do. If I were brave enough to go through with it and my baptism were discovered, it would sink me into deeper water than I'd be able to survive. And no lifeboat would be coming across the waves to rescue what little was left of me. Being baptized in order to follow

Jesus would seal the decision to turn my back on my family, my heritage, my former faith, and everyone from my past whom I knew and loved.

There'd be no turning back.

But what I knew in my heart was that I was *already* too far in to go back. I had no desire to return to Islam. Baptism or not, I had made my decision and had no intention of thinking otherwise. The only decisions to contemplate now were how to plan this public sacrament so that it stayed concealed. And for that, I would need the help of some trusted hands.

By the time I'd selected the right time and location, by the time I'd communicated with the small but secretive guest list, and by the time certain ones had assisted me in thinking through every detail and outcome, the eve of this momentous occasion arrived.

And I was a basket case.

I couldn't allow myself to turn off the lights in my bedroom the entire night. Nerves and anxiety tormented me from one hour to the next, leaving me tossing and turning in a stew of worry. "Lord," I prayed, "You know what I want to do. You know how I love You. But I'm so scared. Please, help me!"

I was relieved by the time the sun peeked over the horizon and my exhausted eyelids succumbed to a desperate few hours of morning sleep. When I awoke shortly thereafter, before my conscious brain had even reminded me what was coming up that day, a passage of memorized Scripture, Galatians 2:20, settled into my spirit: "I have been crucified with Christ; it is no longer I who live, but Christ lives in me; and the life which I now live in the flesh I live by faith in the Son of God, who loved me and gave Himself for me."

It was going to be okay.

I was going to be okay.

The summer day was extraordinary. It couldn't have been more perfect as far as the weather, the temperature, the outdoor conditions. As I arrived at the chosen spot along a creek near (but not too near) my home, a few handpicked witnesses—about twelve people in all—had already gathered. The birds were singing, and the sun shimmered off our faces. Bright green maple leaves danced to the rhythm of the wind. Our fidgety laughter punctuated the air.

Looking down, I smoothed my gorgeous white dress, worn on behalf of the special occasion. It really did feel like a wedding day, and the budding excitement in the crowd only heightened the joyous atmosphere.

People were running late because the location was difficult to find. Not exactly on the beaten path, you know. And since the whole ceremony wouldn't last more than a few minutes from start to finish, I didn't want to proceed until I knew everyone had arrived. Scanning this precious group of friends who'd become like family to me in the space of the past few years, I thought of how often they'd wept with me in my grief and danced with me in my victories. They had risked so much by binding their friendship to mine, and now they were attending one of the biggest moments of all.

Finally, arriving on the scene was the man of the hour: my dear friend Brian. I felt the urge to leap toward him, ecstatic to see this man who'd impacted my spiritual life more profoundly than any other. There was so much in his character, perspective, and demeanor that I wanted to emulate. And there was no one else in the world I would rather have here to baptize me than this incomparable big brother in Christ. I was honored he'd agreed to do it.

And now he was here. Everyone was here. It was time.

And it was picture-perfect.

Tucking my straightened hair behind my ears, I inched out into the water to meet Brian, who'd already positioned himself in a suitable spot. A light breeze kicked into a gusty wind as he began to pray over me, causing the rustling leaves to form sort of a choir around us. Chills shivered through the surface of my skin, even though the water was surprisingly warm. And then my beloved peers in attendance, who'd joined me in the water, reached out to grasp each others' hands, encircling me, singing a song of worship that seemed to draw down all the glories of heaven, funneling God's presence directly into the tiny ring created by our shared fellowship.

As the song ended, I looked up to Brian, whose stature, as always, towered over mine. His eyes were beaming with pride. "We have gathered here today for a glorious moment. This baptism is a public testimony of what has already happened inside Rifqa's heart. This is the day when her decision is sealed as she goes underwater and is baptized in the name of our Lord. You, as her closest friends, are bearing witness to Rifqa's testimony. She is leaving behind family, heritage, and everything she has known to bind herself to Christ Jesus."

He then solemnly but tenderly turned toward me. "Rifqa, do you have anything to say?"

Of course I did.

I delivered a short testimony of my conversion, sharing also a verse I'd memorized for the occasion, ending with that passage from Galatians that God had deposited with such gracious strength and purpose into my mind as I was awakening just that morning.

"So because of your profession of faith in Jesus Christ," Brian concluded, "and in obedience to His command, I baptize you, Rifqa, in His name."

Brian's face blurred as he dipped me with sturdy arms beneath the creek's gently rocking surface. The rush of silence pulsed through my body underwater. *I am dying with You, Lord,* I thought, imagining myself being engulfed into the man Christ Jesus Himself. I came up out of the mass of water to the feeling of electricity jolting my body. *And now I will live with You,* said my abandoned heart, surging back into the summer air, my body drenched in holy acceptance.

I had cemented my eternal vow before all of heaven and earth.

I had wanted truth. And now I was swimming in it.

My mother was too busy cooking to notice my wet hair as I slipped back into the house. By the time she'd turned to see me, I had already ducked inside my room, soon to be completely gone in sleep for the next several hours. The draining emotions of the day had taken everything out of me. And when I woke up to the warmth and stillness of my bed, with darkness already enveloping the room, I cupped my hands behind my head on the pillow and stared up at the blankness of the ceiling above me.

How in the world had all of it worked?

Many things could've gone wrong. There were a lot of moving parts to tie together, without a single one of them springing loose to mar the event or to let on about what I had done. Tumbling the monumental nature of this day over and over in my mind, comparing it with the sullen, surly unhappiness of this place where I slept at night, I marveled at what God had done in my life in such a short yet utterly remarkable time. I felt, in that moment, wholly enjoyed by God. I felt like a different person. Grown up in more ways than my mother and father could ever imagine, who only saw me as someone who was apathetic and indifferent to religious faith.

If they only knew.

But thank God, I was pretty sure they didn't.

Turning to my side to drift back to sleep, I thought back to a mental image from earlier in the day of my friend Michaela holding a special stone in her hand that she gave to me after Brian had lifted me from the water. Under normal circumstances, a baptismal candidate would receive a paper certificate to commemorate the special day, suitable for framing, for scrapbooking, for keeping in a treasured place forever. But for me, the last thing

I could disguise was a piece of paper verifying the date, place, and minister who witnessed my profession of faith in Jesus. The best option, we'd decided, was to inscribe the particulars of my baptism with a marker on a smooth, flat stone and then toss it into the water, where only God and those present would know of its existence.

Revisiting the moment in my mind when that rock splashed down in celebration, before resting at the bottom of the creek bed—my secret faithfully guarded by minnows, crawfish, toads, and beavers—I fell into what almost seemed like a crazy dream. Yet with my lightly damp hair curling across my shoulders, I whispered to myself, "No, Rifqa, you're not dreaming."

I had done it. And now nothing else mattered except the excitement of what my future with Christ might hold.

The stillness I felt in that moment wouldn't hold much longer.

Twelve

I thought for sure I could keep my faith hidden for another two years, long enough to graduate from high school and move to a college far, far from home. Even this plan, I knew, was risky, because my parents could always arrange a marriage for me or simply not let me go to school at all. What would I do then? Who knows? That was for later.

I had more than enough to worry about for now.

One evening a couple of weeks after my baptism, my father's voice boomed outside my bedroom, "Rifqa! Open this d—n door!"

I had just gotten out of the shower and was getting ready for bed. The door was locked, and he was pounding on it, apparently with the back of his fist, the sound becoming increasingly louder with each blow. My heart zoomed to a panicked pulse rate. My whole body began to shake. Where could I hide that he wouldn't find me? I screened the room for a place of safety. *Nowhere.* I had no other choice than to unlock the door.

He burst in as I sank back against the wall, his commanding presence nearly emptying the room of oxygen. I was terrified. Breathless.

"Are you a Christian?!" he screamed.

I didn't answer. What could I say?

"Who is your pastor?!" he asked slightly louder.

I closed my eyes, bracing myself for the beating I knew was coming. *I will not deny You, Lord. I will not deny You, Lord,* I repeated silently to myself, visibly panting. Yet he roared at an even higher volume, continuing with the questions. "Have you been *baptized,* Rifqa?! Answer me!" With my head lowered, eyes glued to the floor, I trembled and said nothing while his body shook and convulsed from an entirely different emotion.

Believe me, I had seen my father angry on dozens and dozens of occasions. Hundreds. But the rage that coursed through him that night, in that instant was like nothing I'd ever seen before. In a flash, he reached for the nearest blunt object, seizing my laptop off the bed and raising it as though he were going to smash it over my head. Everything swirled in slow motion as I caught a glimpse of my mom standing in the distance, watching the entire scene with her arms silently hugging her chest. Her dark brown eyes were filled with tears, not for me, not in horror at my father's assault on his daughter, but in horror at what I had allegedly done to shame the family. She wasn't mourning *his* reaction; she was mourning mine.

Recalibrating my vision on the computer, still cocked in his hand above me but somehow held back from landing its shattering blow, I wished I were already dead. Anything would be better than this.

"If you are a Christian," he yelled, "I am going to kill you! Do you understand?"

Kill me? He couldn't mean it. *Kill me? But Daddy* . . .

Despite how furiously and unpredictably violent he could be, I knew my father wasn't a monster. Looking up into his eyes, so similar in shape and color to mine, I knew he couldn't consider my life so meaningless. Could he? Yet a simple Muslim man who aims to follow his religion must sometimes do the unthinkable to maintain his honor. If that requires sacrificing his rebellious daughter for an offense we both knew to be unforgiveable to him, so be it.

Even seeing him so blinded by rage, I ached in that moment for him to understand and love me, to not be this animal hovering over me. How I wished, too, for my mother to defend and embrace me, to listen to what my heart was saying, to let me melt into her nurturing arms. But what a futile, foolish fantasy. Hatred and contempt of me had completely taken them over. Centuries of disgust seemed etched across my father's face.

"Kill you!" he'd said. "I'm going to kill you!" I had no reason to be-

lieve he wouldn't act on those words. While I wished to be bold and courageous, while I feared being a coward and denying Christ, all I could seem
to do in that moment was tremble, say nothing, and pray this would end
before it turned into a crime scene.

To this day, I'm not sure what distracted him from pummeling my
tiny body with either his fists or my computer. I think, in his own twisted
and mysterious way, he was intending to show me some kind of expression
that equated to mercy in his mind. Even though the night thankfully
ended without my being physically brutalized, his words let me know I
was nearing the end of the road. From this day on, I would never be treated
the same. I was waste to be discarded.

He pointed his finger squarely in my face. "I will give you a few days
to turn back to Islam. I'm going to send you to more Islamic classes. And
I will have mercy on you *if* you give up your faith in Jesus!" But just to be
sure I understood the terms, he added, "You can never have the status of
a true Muslim again since you have done this despicable thing. You are
going to be dead! You understand me? I am giving you mercy now, but if
you do not turn back to Islam, the punishment will be much worse."

The one thing I hadn't done that night in his presence was to declare
myself a Christian. I certainly hadn't *denied* it—but I hadn't said it either.
He didn't quite possess what he needed to follow through on his ultimatum, but he would do it eventually. My upbringing assured me of that. So
I nodded in agreement to everything he told me, eager only to be left alone
and for this firestorm to die down. Acting as though I agreed with him
might buy me some time.

When he finally stomped out of the room, my mind cycled like
radar. *How had he found out? I'd worked so hard to cover my tracks.
Where had I missed it?* I couldn't come up with a hole in my planning. In
all his ranting, he hadn't divulged where he'd gotten the information. I
ran my fingers through my damp hair in a nervous reflex of frustration,

fear, pain, and anxiety. I wanted to scream, but even if I did, no one would hear me.

Everything went downhill after this horrific night of confrontation. My father thankfully went away on one of his business trips, but the ominous air inside the house was more smothering than ever. I wished that I could tell someone what had happened, that I could alert someone to the mortal threat my father had leveled against me, his daughter. But who would ever believe such a thing? How could I get anybody to take me seriously, to think I wasn't exaggerating for attention, that I wasn't embellishing a family argument or maybe covering for some misbehavior that might've justified a parent's unusually angry reaction?

I was walled into a prison of my father's honor and duty. All I could do was keep silent and try to survive it.

If I couldn't scream for help myself, I began secretly hoping that someone would seek me out. Irrational, maybe, but how else was I supposed to think? That's why a few days later, roaming around on Facebook, I leaped at a personal message in my chat box from a woman named Allison. She wasn't anyone I'd ever met, but I knew of her through my connection with the anti-abortion initiative that Brian led. Though she lived in another state, she was good friends with some people I was close to.

Her message had the fingerprints of God all over it: "'Do not fear those who kill the body but cannot kill the soul. But rather fear Him who is able to destroy both body and soul in hell. . . . Whoever confesses Me before men, him I will also confess before My Father who is in heaven. But whoever denies Me before men, him I will also deny before My Father who is in heaven' (Matthew 10:28, 32–33). I just felt like you needed to read this verse today."

Did I ever. Scanning her note again and again, I marveled at the knowledge of God, the power of His Word, and His amazing ability to marshal someone I barely knew—didn't really even know at all—to deliver such a spot-on message to me at an opportune moment. "Do not fear," the verse said, "those who kill the body but cannot kill the soul." My focus needed to be on the One who had claimed me as His own and would defend me as His child.

Allison was right. I couldn't deny Him, even though I realized what this decision entailed on a practical level. My list of available options was shrinking down to one. And if I waited much longer, it would shrink down to none.

Thirteen

Too soon, it was too late. There was no more escape. A friend had invited me to an evening Bible study. "Please, Rifqa. Please come." I hadn't really wanted to chance it. Things were growing more tense at home, and I needed to pick my spots where I thought I could get away from the house unchallenged. Although it was the worst possible timing, something inside urged me on. It was hard to say no, so I acquiesced.

Before the Bible study got underway that night, they spent thirty minutes or more praying over me. I remember it as one of the most intense, strengthening, and affirming moments in my young Christian life. Even though some of them did know the general idea of my story, their prayers that night were inspired with details and particulars that *no one* knew besides me. As with Allison's online message to me from a few weeks before, it was as though we were all attuned to an unseen assault moving into formation against me, and God was giving me (and them) enough inside reporting from the battlefield to keep my spirits up.

I wasn't the only one, however, responding to the buildup. The whole time we were praying, my phone was repeatedly buzzing in my pocket. *My mother was calling.* Which could only mean I'd be answering for this unapproved getaway the minute I walked through the door that night.

I didn't care. It didn't matter anymore. What I needed now was prayer. What I was getting from my Christian friends in that moment was worth whatever I'd be forced to endure when I got home. Yet as soon as I stood to my feet again, I told my friend I needed to leave. Now.

Stepping into the house, the first thing I saw was my mother pacing the floor in agitation. Her eyes were red and swollen from crying. She was obviously waiting to see me. She waved her hands at the sight of my arrival, shouting, "The mosque has been ringing our phones off the hook. They want your father to take care of you or they will have to do it. He's cutting his trip short and coming home this Sunday. How could you bring such shame to us, Rifqa? How?!" she said, slurping a chunk of saliva and spitting it in my face. I felt worse than a dog.

This was as bad as it could get. Now that the mosque leaders had found out about my conversion, it was over. I was done for.

"We are going to send you to Sri Lanka and put you in an *asylum*! Do you hear me? I am packing our bags right now to go," she said. She turned and snatched a little red book from a tabletop and shook it at me. "Why, Rifqa? Why?"

She'd searched my room after the mosque had called, hunting for traces of what her heart feared most. She'd been able to find some corroborating evidence: a Christian book a friend had given me. I hadn't hidden it well enough. I was the one who'd need to be hiding next.

Then without attempting to question me further—assuming my guilt—she yanked my backpack off my arm and plunged her hand inside. I knew exactly what she was looking for. My Bible was secured in a small compartment that wasn't readily accessible. I held my breath as she fished furiously for it. Unsuccessful after several attempts and apparently too flustered to keep trying, she flung the backpack to the floor with a heavy thud, papers and books skidding out haphazardly.

She was right, of course. I was guilty. I didn't even try to mount a defense before her. There had been too many lies and excuses already. I was as tired of my duplicity as she was of my defiance. My love for Christ had been engraved with fire in my heart. It was burning in me, and I couldn't quench the flame. No, I didn't have a good answer for what my next move would be, but it wouldn't be giving in and doing it their way. I had chosen a new way. I had chosen the truth.

And this choice was about to cost me everything.

Just before walking away, my mother looked at me with an awful expression of grief and bewilderment and said with disdainful finality, "I am sorry that I gave birth to you."

That weekend was the closest to hell on earth I had ever lived. My mother, after venting her heartbreak and anger, refused to talk or even look at me. My existence had become a disgrace to her, my father, my family. Death and pain seemed to lurk in every corner, in every noise and pop and unexpected sound. I sat alone in my room the rest of that night, petrified, agonizing at the thought of my father bursting in the door from his jewelry exhibition, having been forced to return early—something he'd never, ever done—to exact his revenge.

How had the mosque found out about me? I had no idea. Surely my dad hadn't told them. He would never have wanted them to know. He would've done anything to avoid being publicly shamed by having a daughter who'd become a Christian. All I could figure was that somehow my Facebook postings—which I'd been so careful to keep private, to keep obscure, to say nothing while saying everything—had not been discreet enough. Someone must have been tracking me and had ratted me out.

I barely slept that night, feeling the tick of each minute that stood between me and my father's angry return. At least I had a day to think of something, assuming my mother's pronouncement of his itinerary was accurate. It wasn't much time. Whatever I was going to do, I needed to do it quickly.

On Saturday I decided I had nothing to lose. If this were truly the last day before my dad came home to do whatever he intended to do to me, I needed to make the most of it. So I lied to my mother, telling her I was going to work, but instead I caught a ride to a prayer room in downtown Columbus run by some of the campus ministry people at Ohio State whom I'd met through Brian. They called it a prayer room, but it was actually a rental house focused almost entirely on giving kids a place to spend time with the Lord and each other. They'd sometimes have meetings there if people needed a central gathering point. But it was primarily focused on establishing a culture of prayer. It wasn't uncommon for somebody to show up just wanting to pray, to get off by themselves, to swirl paint on big pieces of paper available for freestyle worship and expression. It was not only common; this was why it existed.

The prayer room was too far away for me to visit often. And because I didn't have a car or driver's license at the time, I was dependent on other people to take me there. On this day in particular, I didn't know where else to go.

I spent most of the day locked away in a room by myself, praying, sobbing, wailing. The terror of my reality hung over me like a lead weight, knifing into my soul. The dread of being physically harmed, perhaps even taken to Sri Lanka against my will, as my mother had said, pressed down on me with its full weight. If I didn't think of an alternative in the next twelve to twenty-four hours, I'd be giving somebody else the authority to do all my thinking *for* me. It would be out of my hands at that point. When time ran out tomorrow, I couldn't just be sitting here without a plan, unprepared. I had to be ready. Or not be found.

I couldn't believe it had come to this.

Alone, tormented, I remember spying myself in a nearby mirror, hardly recognizing the young woman staring back at me. She didn't look sixteen; she looked aged, drawn, fractured . . . old. My normally brown face was oddly pale, and the raw puffiness around my eyes rendered them dull and lifeless. My curly dark hair was wound into a messy bun with strands sticking out everywhere. She was a frightening picture to look at, this girl, this woman. Refusing to let her masquerade as me, I forced a smile in her direction to shatter her haggard image.

I wasn't going to be defined by people who could drive me to this state, even if they were my parents, even if they were leaders of the mosque who hid their hatred and fear behind their religious authority. I was afraid of them, yes. They'd succeeded at that. But Christ was beckoning my frightened spirit to trust Him and surrender. I wasn't facing this valley of death alone. He would show me what to do and would somehow carry me through it.

Darkness had fallen by the time I got home. My friend let me out of the car several blocks away—a tactic I'd been forced to employ each time somebody picked me up or dropped me off. My father wasn't home yet—thank God—but the air inside our little apartment was charged with a silent sense of apprehension, anger, and animosity. My mother, sitting on the couch, worked hard not to acknowledge my presence. That suited me fine. The less anybody acknowledged me, the better.

I walked to my room, closed the door, and just sat there—prayerful yet indecisive—as the anxiety of the evening wore on. The later the hour grew, the more my churning emotions urged me to action. Totally at the end of my wits, I fumbled for my phone and began punching in a familiar number. Brian's. I knew he would do everything in his power to help protect me and, more than anyone else I could think of, would understand and give me counsel on what to do.

He answered. *Whew.* I immediately began, through frantic whispers, to tell him what was going on. As I'd done with Katie, I still couldn't say everything—couldn't say I was on a death watch—for fear of sounding melodramatic. So again I muted the risk, telling him my parents were threatening to kick me out of the house. Surely that was enough to register the seriousness of my situation without just being told to calm down.

When I finally gave him time to speak, his voice was smooth and confident. "You're fine, Rifqa. This is America. They won't kick you out," he said matter-of-factly.

I knew Brian meant well and was trying to comfort me, and part of me wanted to believe he was right. Yet I knew he was ignorant of the world I came from. He was an African American, a pastor's kid, raised all his life in the freedoms of this country. How could he possibly understand the consequences of my repressive culture? How could I expect him to comprehend the fear I lived in every day, even *before* my conversion, much less afterward? He didn't know how it felt to be a young Muslim woman with no rights to my own thoughts and desires, with no recourse from the religious tyranny of my family. *Why did I even think he would understand?*

"I'm sure you'll be okay," he said. "I'll Skype you later tonight to check up on you."

I thanked him before disengaging, trying to project a brave face. I swallowed the confirmation of my worst suspicions. No one was going to believe me. Everyone felt so far away.

Even God.

So I started to pack. I didn't know what else to do. It sure beat sitting there and awaiting the inevitable. I tugged clothes off hangers from the closet and stuffed them into bags. I looked through drawers and under the bed, trying to determine my bare essentials—precious diaries and belongings, must-haves if I truly decided to run. The more stuff I gathered together, the more urgently I felt time slipping away. Time. Time. Time. I didn't have much time!

Then my eyes fell on a picture. A photo of the little man who'd won my heart and wrapped me around his little finger. *Rajaa,* I whispered brokenly. Dropping whatever I was holding, I pulled the picture of my little brother toward me. There we were, the two of us together, smiling for the camera, his innocent grin belying his fiery personality. I was holding him so close that my hair nearly covered him, the way I wished my love could reach out and cover him now. A sword of pain tore through my heart as I thought about the prospect of never seeing my little brother again. Tears welled in my eyes. I wanted to break down and sob. I didn't know if I could go through with this anymore. I didn't know if it was even worth it anymore; the hurt and anguish seemed to swallow me.

I laid his picture down and slinked into the hushed, darkened living room, totally spent, totally at the end.

I hadn't eaten. I hadn't slept. I felt weak beyond words. A strike of pain, in fact, like lightning, suddenly shot up my leg—a physical manifestation, I suppose, of the enormous stress I was under. It hit me everywhere. My muscles tightened into a knot of discomfort, refusing to ease.

I tried deep breathing, keenly aware of my need to stay quiet. I tried pacing a little, walking it off, seeing if the pain would subside. My mother and Rajaa were the only ones home, and both of them were asleep in her bedroom. I couldn't afford to wake them.

With each wincing step, while I cried inside to keep from giving the pain an audible moan, my heart began to sing the worship theme that ate into my fears and motivated me to action: I had decided to follow Jesus, and I wouldn't turn back. Alone against the world, alone toward the cross, I was taking my stand.

And there was no turning back.

After gathering myself enough to return to my room, I saw from the clock by my bedside that it was after midnight. Brian hadn't checked back. It was too late to call anyone. I opened my computer and scrolled onto Facebook, hoping against hope, like the night Allison had written me, that God had quickened someone's interest enough to reach out to me even at this odd, inexplicable hour.

Amazingly, again the notification of a new message *did* appear. I clicked the icon. "Beverly Lorenz," I quietly read aloud as I saw her picture and post. I had heard Brian mention this name before on numerous occasions as being the mother of his recent roommate. My only interaction with her had been as part of a conference call with people from around the nation, praying for a young lady who was proceeding with an abortion.

Many of the participants on that phone call had become Facebook friends with each other, including Beverly with me. But that was the sum total of what I knew about her.

Her simple note to me stirred my soul: "There is a wall of fire surrounding you. He is your shield! I am praying for you."

How had she known? At this late hour? Maybe Brian had told her. I gaped at the timing of her comment. Enlarging her picture, I saw her with a man I assumed to be her husband. They looked warm and welcoming. Even strangers felt safe in a desperate moment like this. Though I'd never met this person and could only vaguely remember the sound of her voice, I felt a strange tug of desire urging me to tell her what was happening. Tell Beverly. Whoever and wherever she was.

"Can you please call me?" I typed to her in a private message.

Almost immediately she answered. "Yes."

So I entered my cell phone number and pushed Send, then sat on the edge of my seat, awaiting her call.

Fifteen minutes later, I was still waiting. Sweating. I punched around on my phone to be sure it was powered on. It was. *What was the matter?*

Checking my laptop again, I saw another message from her: "Your phone is disconnected. I tried calling. Here's *my* number . . ."

Weird. My phone had worked earlier. I'd talked with Brian on it just a few hours before. All I could figure was that my father had disconnected it, and the cancellation of service had probably taken effect at midnight. If so, I was beginning to lose all ability to get help. My lines of communication were dwindling. I knew now, for my safety's sake, if I could possibly reach Beverly from our home line, I needed to tell her the whole truth and not sugarcoat anything.

So I crept from my room, lifted the cordless phone from its cradle, and took it out on the balcony. The other handset, I knew, was in my mother's room, and if she heard me talking and picked up, she'd hear every word. But I didn't have time to confine this conversation to back-and-forth Facebook messages. I had no choice but to risk it. *Lord, please keep my mother asleep. Please, oh, please, don't let her wake up. Help me, Father!*

It took a few tries at dialing, because my hands were shaking too much to hit the right buttons. Finally I got it to ring through. Someone answered on the other end.

"Hello, Rifqa!" A sweet southern voice cheerfully greeted me.

"Hi, Beverly."

"What's going on, sweetie?"

I started crying uncontrollably the minute she asked the question. "I am so scared . . ." My head was pounding, but nothing held me back in that moment. In less than two minutes, I told her about my conversion to Christianity, my father's threats, and how he was coming home later today to "take care" of me. I told her all of it. All the atrocity of it.

I don't know what she actually heard. I'm sure my story completely blindsided her. She counseled me to calm down and take a few deep breaths. She could tell I was panicking, and she offered to stop right then and pray for me.

I loved that she would do that. But I already felt like it was too late for me. What could she really do to help this trembling voice on the phone line in the middle of the night? So I said to her, summoning up what little courage I could muster, "Will you pray that in the face of death I will not deny Jesus?"

A still, buzzing silence was all I could hear on the phone.

"Hello?" I said, shaken. "Are you still there?"

"Yes, sweetie, I'm still here."

"I'm sorry, I just—"

"Listen, Rifqa, I live in Florida, but my home is open to you, okay? I really mean that."

I knew she did. Even though she was a stranger, I could tell she was absolutely genuine. But even compassion like hers couldn't really help me right then. Nothing could help me. Yet at least somebody knew. At least

I'd finally been able to tell somebody. Feeling the encouragement of her prayer echoing through the phone would need to be enough for me.

She said her "amen"—that little word that could still excite me just as it had first intrigued me at Aiden's house years before. Terrified of being caught by my mother talking on the balcony in the middle of the night, I said a hurried goodbye, hung up, and reentered my lonely, dark world.

Fourteen

It was about 3:00 a.m. when I ended the conversation with Beverly, replaced the phone, and returned to the quiet of my bedroom. No one had heard me. Flipping open my laptop, I updated my Facebook status with an ominous line: "Packing my bags . . ." Then I sat down weakly on the floor, my head buried in my hands. "Jesus . . . ," I whispered again and again, a bottomless groan brimming over from within my spirit. Saying His name was the only prayer I could offer anymore. I was pleading for Him to save me as though I was praying with my last breath.

A faint electronic sound roused me, reclaiming my attention. I held my breath and listened closer. Standing up, I looked around, sure that I'd heard it again. Then I saw the Skype program on my computer flashing brightly with a fresh alert: "Brian calling."

Pressing the answer button, I whispered sharply to him, "I can't talk. My mother's sleeping in the next room. Let's type and talk." Without waiting for his response, I ended the call. His image blinked away.

I rubbed my hand against my forehead, edgy about being overheard and discovered. I hated living such a guarded life. But under the circumstances, chatting with Brian was probably a better way to settle my nerves than anything else I could do, as long as I typed very quietly.

"I saw the update on your status," he wrote, "and got worried. Are you really leaving, Rifqa?"

"No . . . I'm not. But I want to."

"Do you really think your dad is going to kick you out? This is America! You're underage. It's against the law."

So, as with Beverly, with nothing else to lose, I gave it to him straight, whether he believed it or not.

"You're being too dramatic," he answered after reading the truth of it.

"Do you think it's a joke, Brian?" I wrote, beginning to steam at his lack of understanding, to the point of feeling betrayed, sick of having to fight so hard against these forces of injustice everywhere. "There are hundreds of men and women that die for the gospel every day in other countries. Do you think they're faking it when they're slaughtered at the hands of their oppressors? When they cry out for help from their brothers and sisters, is that 'being too dramatic'?!"

I knew by the silence on the other end that he was hearing me. Finally. The screen indicated he was typing a response, so I waited eagerly. When his words appeared, they weren't the ones I was expecting.

"You need to leave now."

Was he serious?

Then this: "I'm coming to get you."

Wait, though. I knew he was out of town, taking a sabbatical at a huge church a couple of states away. It was already Sunday morning by then, practically sunrise. My father would be home within hours. I didn't know when, but soon. Very soon. I didn't have time to wait for Brian to get here. If I was leaving, it really did need to be *now*.

As illogical as his ultimatum seemed to be, it did feel good to know he was finally hearing me. Maybe he could help me think of something.

"Brian, my mother is going to be up really soon. I can't wait that long. Can you have someone pick me up and take me somewhere?"

He replied swiftly. "I'll call a taxi for you." He said he'd instruct them to take me to a particular church—one of the biggest ones in town—where I'd be able to blend in without being noticed. "Just stay there until I come get you. Don't go anywhere else."

I felt the adrenaline pulsing through my body. This was really happening.

"Where will you take me from there?" I asked, trying to hide my concern.

"I'm talking to a lady named Beverly Lorenz right now. I'm going to see if you can go stay with them."

Beverly? The lady I was just talking to? For the first time, a wave of hopeful excitement rushed over me. It sounded too good to be true. Could I really go someplace like Beverly's where I could live in freedom and safety? Somewhere I could practice my faith openly without needing to hide and outmaneuver people? I could not believe what I was reading.

I couldn't daydream for long. I needed to leave.

Another ding sounded from my computer. "Write your parents a letter," Brian said, "telling them you're leaving. I'll meet you at the church. Don't talk to anyone or even look at anyone! Keep to yourself, Rifqa."

Brian was risking everything to help me escape. I couldn't believe it. Why would anybody be willing to do all this for me?

Streaks of morning light were peeking through my window when our conversation ended. I couldn't delay the inevitable any longer. Time was taunting me, and soon it would be too late to escape. A vivid statement, in fact, came to me as I sat there, as if hand-delivered from the Holy Spirit: *Leave your father's house, Rifqa. Follow Me. I will be the Lord your God.* It wasn't just a wish; it was Him. My God was leading me onward.

With that, I was up and on the move.

I tore out a piece of paper and prepared to put into words what I'd been hiding from my family for nearly four years. My hands were trembling almost too violently to write. The lack of sleep, the lack of nourishment, the physical pain, even if slightly numbed into the background—all of it was working against me. Quickly I scratched the following words onto the page:

Jesus Christ is my Lord and Savior. I refuse to deny Him, nor will I ever. I pray and hope you find His mercy and forgiveness. Love you both dearly.
—Rifqa

I couldn't even take time to reread the words. The only thing on my mind was leaving. Picking up my backpack from the corner, I unzipped it and slipped in my laptop plus the book I was reading, my journal, and my cell phone and charger. Even though my phone had been cut off, I didn't want my father to have access to my contacts or anything else on the device. I glanced at the bag of clothes and stuff I'd been packing several hours before and prepared to start weeding out what should stay and what should go. The choices seemed too much to process for my splintered mind. That's when I made the snap decision. Just leave it. Leave it all. The extra weight would only slow me down. Besides, there was something almost symbolic about abandoning the whole lot of it. I was leaving everything behind to follow Jesus—spiritually, emotionally, and now physically. Forsaking it all. Leaving with nothing but my backpack and the clothes on my back.

So this was it. This was where it ended and where so many unknowns splayed out before me, making sense only by the knowledge that God Himself would be in charge of it all. It would be hard; I was sure of that. However, it wouldn't be whatever death sentence my father was racing home to mete out. I at least had a head start on a free life.

But not if I didn't leave right then.

I took one last look around the room, again stopping at the photo of my little brother. I stared at his big brown eyes, missing him already and praying he would one day understand why I'd needed to do this. I silently said my goodbyes, closed my eyes, and grieved at the heartbreaking memories. Once more, I reached out to pick up Rajaa's picture, but I couldn't do it. I could only groan as I forced myself to step away.

After quickly making my bed, I set the note to my parents neatly and visibly by the pillow. I glanced out my window, where the sun was colorfully announcing the time of day, illuminating the path to my freedom. Turning away from the window, I twisted the knob of my bedroom door and slowly pushed it open. Thankfully no one else was up.

I tiptoed into the hallway, scanning for any signs of wakefulness or motion. With each hollow step through the living room, I was cognizant of all I was leaving behind: my culture, my family, my identity, my religious heritage, my memories, perhaps even my future. I quietly twisted the knob on the front door, opened it, then couldn't seem to prevent it from slamming noisily behind me. I didn't care. I had to leave. I ran from building to building, zigzagging my way out of our apartment complex.

My journey to freedom had just begun.

Fifteen

Ten minutes passed.

Twenty minutes passed.

Forty minutes passed.

Nothing.

The only thing barely shielding me from discovery (if my mother was already looking for me) was the large tree trunk I was hiding behind. Hunched into a ball on the ground, I wondered if I'd missed seeing the taxi come by. Maybe it had already come and gone. How was I supposed to know where to be looking for it?

The morning chill cut through my frail body, nerve endings already twitchy and on edge. Shivering, I rubbed the arms of my thin brown sweater and tried to stay warm. As time stretched on, I couldn't help feeling swallowed by anger and helplessness. I'd put all my hope in God, and this is what I was getting in return? Waiting for help that wasn't showing up? Sneaking around like a criminal? I had been gone from home nearly an hour yet was still dangerously close to our apartment property, with no one to help me and no clue what to do next.

By this time the intermittent bursts of faith and bravery that I'd felt the night before were all gone. Picking up pebbles and loose gravel that were sprinkled around me, I flicked them with anger toward the sky. "You said You would protect me! You said You would lead me! *Where are you?!*"

The next thought that breathed through the air, however, with some of my nervous energy now expended, was a stream of inspiration through Scripture: *By faith, Rifqa. By faith Abraham obeyed when he was called. And he went out not knowing where he was going. By faith*—a passage I recognized from Hebrews 11, a listing of heroes from the Bible. Immediately I knew what I was supposed to do. Faith requires action, and the time for action was now.

So I decided to start walking.

Dusting the dirt off my backpack, I stood to my feet. My green dress was wrinkled and stained from the ground, and my muddy legs epitomized the muddled state I was in. But what I looked like didn't matter. What mattered was getting a move on.

I spun my back to the apartment buildings and walked toward the adjoining street. Soon my brisk pace sped into a jog and then a runner's sprint. My lungs started to burn as the backpack thumped and pounded me with every step. By the time I approached a residential area, I was panting and drained.

Then, like a snap of sudden insight, I knew exactly where to go. *Katie's house.* She'd told me on the bus that I could come there if I needed to, and I'd never needed to get anywhere more desperately than I did now. It had been years, though, since I'd actually visited her house. I only barely remembered where it was and what it looked like. I couldn't remember the street name. But I knew it was around here somewhere.

"Lord, help me!" I pleaded.

It was 6:30 by this time, maybe later. For all I knew, my father could be showing up at home any minute. And from there his first move would be to drive around and scan the sidewalks. I was hardly inconspicuous—a sixteen-year-old Sri Lankan girl walking around in a dress and backpack on an early Sunday morning. So while the focus I needed for locating Katie's house required a lot of my attention, I also needed to stay alert for my father. He might be looking for me already.

The only thing that registered with me as I continued swiveling my head back and forth, trying to place which house belonged to the Jacobs family, was a white car ahead of me, parked in the driveway. Drawing closer, I could hear its engine running, but no one was inside. Looking at the house directly in front of it, I felt an inner urge that told me I was in the right spot, that I needed to approach. The house looked vaguely familiar, but I still wasn't sure. Suddenly, after hardly setting foot on the driveway, I spotted a black woman behind the glass door.

Katie's mom!

At the sight of her face, I bolted up the walk as she spun the door open—a bright, loving smile on her face. I started to cry, barely able to speak. I knew I looked like a madwoman, with my windblown hair and muddy legs. I lunged into the entrance of her home anyway, sobbing uncontrollably, stating emphatically, "I've got to get to the church! I've got to get to the church!"

"Sure, honey," she said, surprisingly calm. "I'll help you." I told her which church I meant. "Okay," she said as she hurriedly gathered her purse. "I've been up waiting here for you since four o'clock. The Lord told me you would come. I was just about to give up and leave, but I came back in the house when I realized I'd forgotten my purse."

Really? Seriously? It made no sense.

By faith, Rifqa . . . By faith . . .

We both ran out of the house, and I dove into the car as fast as I could. Without explaining why, I ducked my head under the dashboard, wondering what she must be thinking but not wanting to take the time to tell the whole story. Maybe Katie had told her some of it. I hoped she knew how to find this church, because I sure didn't. I'd never been there before.

"Do you need me to drop off food anywhere?" she asked me. "Is there anything else I can do to help you?" But that's all the inquisition she made into my bizarre behavior. Her generosity and kindness made me want to weep. "No, thank you," I said, inching my head up enough to peek out the window. I could see the church in the distance. "Thank you for doing this," I gushed, preparing to make a fast exit. Then as we slowed and I got out of the car, I looked back at Mrs. Jacobs and said, "Thank you! Thank you!" over and over. I wondered if I'd ever see her again as I hugged her goodbye one last time.

Sprinting toward the entrance to the church building, I felt like I was leaving my dark world of oppression behind. A sense of liberation coursed through my body. I could go in here and scream "Jesus!" as loud as I wanted, and nobody—not my father, not my family, not the Imam himself—could stop me!

The door was unlocked so I stepped in. It was about 7:30. The lobby that led into an elegant hall was mostly quiet and vacant. I knew I wasn't home free, but at least I'd made it this far, and I was in a lot better shape than I'd been an hour before. Prancing into the large, open hallway, I said at half-volume, "I'm free!"—delirious at hearing my words dance off the walls and echo back around me. I couldn't believe what I was feeling. I didn't need to hide or be quiet. I squealed with delight.

But it was going to be a long wait. This place was going to be my hideout for the day. So I climbed the stairs and found a small table in the empty church balcony. From there I had a clear view of the entrance doors, where hopefully Brian would soon appear.

Over the course of the next few hours a number of busy Sunday services started and ended. No one had done much more than wave and say hello to me. I was glad of that. I certainly wasn't here to get on the mailing list or be trotted around like a Sunday school visitor. By early afternoon the last of the crowds had dwindled to barely a handful of people, and the sky visible through the front windows had darkened to a gloomy gray. I hopped off the table and peered around, trying to figure where I needed to go to keep from looking like a squatter and yet not venture too far from the front door.

For a moment I thought I'd slip alone into the sanctuary. I was enraptured by the size and spaciousness of it. I wondered if any of the thousands of worshipers that morning had been as hungry to enter this place as I was.

Did they realize what a privilege they had to enjoy, to actually walk into the house of God and praise Him without the slightest hindrance? I sat on a seat near the back and took off my shoes. The cool carpet rubbed against my feet. It felt good. Then I pulled my legs up and wrapped my arms around my knees, staring with disbelieving wonder into the large, darkened auditorium. Faint light from the stormy sky blanketed the room in softness and silence, and my whole body relaxed under a covering of momentary peace.

Hours ticked by. No movement. No Brian. Just me and God, alone with a lifetime of thoughts. In between runs of free-flowing prayer and worry, I found myself thinking of little Rajaa, saddened at the notion of missing out on his precious life, maybe forever. I even thought of my mother—her big brown eyes and her lips that looked so much like mine. I was often very afraid of her, and yet I strangely found myself missing her, enough that I shamelessly wept while the empty room echoed my grief. Would I ever see her again? Of course not. This path to freedom only led one way, and going home wasn't on its flight plan.

Sixteen

Whirrrrrr! The maintenance man had begun his Sunday after-noon routine, the roar of his industrial vacuum cleaner nosing its way closer to where I was sitting. I'm sure he had no idea why I was weep-ing and whimpering. But he acted like he didn't want to notice. Tending to someone like me, I'm sure, wasn't on his methodical schedule, and prob-ably not within his skill set anyway. His arrival on the scene let me know I needed to find another place to hide. I didn't want to be forced to explain to the cleaning crew or security guards what I was doing here alone in church.

Just then it dawned on me that I hadn't slept in more than thirty hours. I was as much a physical wreck as an emotional and mental one. So as I slipped out of the sanctuary and into the hallway, I began hunting a place where I might be able to lay my head down and sleep. I still wanted to stay alert to Brian's arrival, but fatigue was coming close to incapacitat-ing me. I was famished, running on my last dregs of energy.

Stopping by a bathroom, finding no one inside, I locked myself in a large handicapped stall and practically crumpled to the ground, my weak and bony legs shivering at the touch of the cold tile floor. Of all the things I never saw myself doing, one of them included taking a nap in a rest room. Running away from home to avoid the possibility of being killed was once on that dreaded list as well, and I'd already crossed that one off this morn-ing. So ignoring my shame and the chill in my body, I curled into a ball in a corner of the stall. I used my backpack for a pillow and closed my tear-filled eyes. Who would rescue me? I fell asleep to the whisper of my own voice, crying, "Lord, save me . . ."

I didn't sleep for as long as it seemed, but the short nap somewhat energized me. By the time I emerged from the ladies' room—apparently undetected—I felt a little better. A little sharper. I decided to go back upstairs to the seclusion of the balcony, where I'd positioned myself at first. I could occasionally hear people coming and going from there, but as of yet, no sign of Brian.

Where is he? I wondered, growing more nervous and edgy with each passing hour. *What if he never shows up? What should I do then?* I couldn't seem to sit still with these thoughts for very long without wanting to jump out of my skin. So at intervals I'd get up and walk around, trying to clear my head, trying to settle myself down.

Finally I heard my name.

"Rifqa!"

I stopped in my tracks. I ran and peered over the balcony. "Hello?" I said meekly. No one was there.

"Rifqa!"

I knew I wasn't hearing things. "Yes? Hello?" Gripping my hands to the railing so I could lean over a little farther, I thought I glimpsed someone in a white-and-brown striped dress shirt—the kind I'd seen Brian frequently wearing. I craned my neck even more, my hair hanging loosely down to the side. But before I could catch a closer look, he'd disappeared.

"Brian?"

It must not have been him, I thought. *He wouldn't have just left like that.* But I didn't have a working cell phone. I was completely out of contact. Our only system of communication consisted of hoping we'd run into each other.

What I'm about to write may strike you as impossible, and I can't prove it beyond all doubt except by telling you I know for sure it happened.

As the swelling of fear caused my heart to absolutely burst with hopelessness, I sensed the Presence again. No one was there, but *Someone* was there. I could feel a gaze burning through me. I was so sure, in fact, that I dared only to turn my head slowly from the railing when I became aware of it, almost afraid to look in its direction. The empty air revealed no form, no substance. Yet from a totally unknown source and out of all context with the lonely, abandoned reality of my situation, my heart began to burn with an indescribable sense of warmth and safety. An angel was disguised within the darkened doorway. I knew it as certainly as I knew every detail of that second-floor balcony, having spent the bulk of the day growing oddly familiar with the stretch of carpet and pieces of furniture.

And once again I was assured in my spirit that my God was watching over me.

The rest of the afternoon and early evening brought no news of Brian. I sat in the dark of the balcony, quiet and hidden from view, and sweated out an unknown future that so far was not going smoothly at all. I could only imagine what had happened at home earlier that day, both when my mother had awakened and noticed I was gone, or when my father had arrived, ready for action. I didn't see any way they could find me here. A large area church may not have been the last place they'd think to look, but it wouldn't have been the first. I was pretty sure I was safe here— from *them,* at least.

Repeatedly checking the time, I watched the clock tick past seven, past eight, past nine, past ten. The whole church was totally empty, except for one or two uniformed security guards who apparently were part of a small round-the-clock force. It was now eleven o'clock. Still no sight of Brian. Either I'd missed him before—by a maddening few yards and seconds—or he had somehow been detained and had never gotten here. Like it or not, I needed to think on my feet. It was pretty clear by this time: no one was coming for me that night. I couldn't stay here forever. The guards downstairs were bound to find me and question me before they locked up.

With the decision bearing down hard, a passing memory came to mind just as I was standing up: an online message I'd received from a Facebook friend named Alana. She'd described for me a dream where I was being dragged away by two police officers. In her dream, she told me, I opened my mouth and a trumpet came out of it. Once the trumpet was blown, all of heaven came down to save me.

I knew from reading the Bible that whenever a trumpet sounded in Scripture, it usually meant one of two things: either the people of God were being gathered to pray or the nation was being rallied for war.

Standing there, spurred on by the need to take action, this obscure dream seemed to be saying something to me. I was certain, of course, that Brian had mobilized my church friends to pray, and I knew a war was set to begin over my physical and spiritual rights. So it was time, I felt, to bring this whole dream-like imagery to life.

I was ready to approach the two security men and ask for help.

My feet were tingling from sitting still for so long as I slowly walked downstairs to speak with them. The head officer, who seemed about three times my size, took a long, inquiring look at me.

"Who are you? What are you doing here?"

I clung to my renewed boldness, but it was fading fast.

"Where are your parents, young lady? How old are you?"

I thought about lying, claiming to be older, but I couldn't do it. "Uh, sixteen," I sputtered.

The officer scooted a phone across the desk toward me. "Call your parents, please."

He didn't look mean. Just concerned. Yet forceful.

My only hope of this turning out well was in telling the truth—mostly. "My parents are Muslim. They can't know I'm here. I'll go home tomorrow, but they can't find out I was here tonight."

"Muslim, huh," he said, his reaction suddenly changing. "I was just reading the other day," pulling a magazine from behind his desk, "this article right here." Flipping to it, he started reading aloud, with obvious interest, about the dangers of Muslims converting out of Islam.

What did this mean? Was he going to be sympathetic toward me? Would he be willing to help me?

"Can you take me to my friend's house?" I asked. I'm sure my face looked desperate as I held my breath, awaiting a response. He paused for a few seconds, then turned and motioned for me to follow him. He led me outside, not saying much, where he opened the back door of his patrol car and told me to hop in.

"So, what's your name, miss?" he asked as he started the car and looked back at me in his rearview mirror.

"Anna Michelle," I told him, using the alias my Christian friends used for me. I didn't want to tell him my real name, not wanting to provide my parents any more of a trace on my whereabouts.

"What's your address?"

"Thirteen thirty-four Cherry Bottom Street." I made that up too.

"And where are we going? Where's your friend's house?"

I couldn't believe it. He was actually going to take me to safety. I shivered as I felt the same Presence I had sensed in the church balcony, protecting me, caring for me, positioned right next to me, unseen in the backseat. I hoped he also came with a good sense of direction, because I didn't really know how to get to Katie's house from there. I led the officer on a few wrong turns and was feeling more lost by the second.

"You really need to know where you're going," he told me, sounding a little peeved and impatient, maybe beginning to wonder if I was conning him.

I was starting to get nervous. The houses were hard to distinguish in the dark. "I'm sorry, sir, I've just never gone there from this route." If I couldn't find it soon, I didn't know what he would do with me.

"There it is! That's it! That's the house," I yelled, as it finally came into view. Rolling his cruiser to a stop on the street out front, the guard looked at me and smiled. "The person who lives here is a cop. You see that car?"

he said, pointing to a blue sedan in the driveway. "That's an officer's license plate."

"Really?" I said. Uh-oh. Didn't know that.

"Listen," he said, spinning around to look into my eyes before turning the engine off. "I'm not really allowed to do this because you're a minor. But I'm trusting you. You'll go home tomorrow night, right?"

Gritting my teeth, I said, "Yes sir." I hated lying.

"Good girl. Come on."

You're a good man, I thought to myself. *You have no idea you're saving my life by doing this.*

We walked up the driveway together, and he rang the doorbell. My heart was racing, fearing what would happen if no one answered. Within moments, the thick green door swung open and Katie's mom appeared. Her lips broke into a smile as I lunged into her comforting embrace.

She whispered to me, "I knew you would be back."

"Do you know her?" asked the security guard.

"Yes sir. I do," she said, holding me.

"Okay, good night then." He left as quickly as he came. Once again, God had put the right person in my path at the right time. *By faith, Rifqa . . . By faith . . .*

But my parents were still only blocks away. I hadn't gotten far after a whole day of trying. "I can't be here!" I said to Mrs. Jacobs. "I have to go! I've got to get out of here!"

The lights were only dimly lit in the Lorenz home as Beverly listened again to the unanswered ring of Brian's cell phone. To her anxious disappointment, the call rolled over to voice mail for what seemed like the hundredth time.

Hanging up without leaving another message, she stared blankly through the window into the late-night Florida sky. Her motherly heart ached with concern, wondering what was going on with me and with Brian.

"Where are they?" she whispered, agonizing, beginning to fear the worst. *What if Rifqa's dad has gotten hold of both of them?*

Seventeen

I t was late, but Mrs. Jacobs could tell I was frantic by the way I was running around, refusing to sit still. I just kept repeating, "I can't be here!"
Her husband, the policeman, wasn't at home. (Probably good for me.) So
after she came up with a plan. "Tell you what, Rifqa. I'll take you to my
mom's house. Katie is there. It's an hour away."

I knew I was being a real inconvenience, but I couldn't care. I had no
other choice than to be right here where I was, and I needed her help more
than I needed to be polite. But what about Brian? Now that our plans had
changed, how would he know where to find me? Continuing to intrude, I
asked if I could use her phone to call my friend who'd been supposed to
pick me up earlier in the day.

He wasn't answering. I couldn't understand it. Maybe he just didn't
recognize the number and couldn't risk taking the call. My only other
hope of reaching him—of reaching somebody—was through Beverly. So
after retrieving her number from my backpack, I tried her line. She answered immediately.

"Rifqa! Where are you? Are you okay? Where *are* you?" Beverly's
voice was part relief, part questions.

"Brian never came," I said. "I don't know where he is," explaining that
I was safe with a friend but needed to leave immediately to get farther out
of town.

"Oh, I've been worried sick," she said. "I've been trying to reach him
too. I'm so glad you're all right."

Pacified by her voice and concern, I at least didn't feel quite so panicky
anymore. We both agreed to wait and hope to hear from Brian the next
morning, since there was nothing more we could do until he called Beverly

back. I told her where I was going and said I'd be in touch. Hearing her sweet voice again made me so excited. I couldn't *wait* to get to Florida!

By the time we reached Katie's grandma's house, it was one or two in the morning, but my friend was up and waiting for me. What a luxury to see her face and be enveloped by her love after the traumatic day I'd been through. It also felt good to be that much farther from my parents and know I could sleep through the rest of the night without fear. Snuggling under the silky bed sheets a half hour later, I gave into the warmth of the moment. I hadn't felt this way in a long time.

The instant my eyelids opened, I was in a state of hysteria. My hands tensely clutched the sheets as the thought *Where am I?* sprinted across my mind. I breathed a sigh of relief upon the realization of where I was.

I was safe.

The warmth of the sunlight felt calming as it touched my face and skin. It felt like a new day. As I drank in the serenity, unexpected tears began to trickle down my face. My tears became apologetic sobs at the realization that I was grasping to save my life. I ached to be brave and bold for Christ, but I was instead whimpering under the fear of my earthly father holding the power to take my life. In that moment, I thought again about how I had relinquished my life to Christ. I had not left my family and identity just to be alive. I had left everything I had ever known to follow Jesus Christ and love Him forever. His presence started filling the room as I heard the ever-so-familiar voice whispering, *He who finds his life will lose it, and he who loses his life for My sake will find it.* I was so scared. Yet a new sense of confidence in God's perfect leadership over my life was awakened.

I was not the one conducting the show. He was.

My survival wasn't dependent on me but on Him.

So I decided to start living like it and embrace the powerful words of one of my biblical heroes: Esther.

She was a Jewish orphan raised by her uncle Mordecai in the land of Persia. Through a series of divine circumstances, she was chosen to be the wife of King Ahasuerus. Her faith in Yahweh was a secret. In the powerful story, a decree was sent throughout the land for the death of all the Jews.

Mordecai said to Esther, "Do not think in your heart that you will escape in the king's palace any more than all the other Jews. For if you remain completely silent at this time, relief and deliverance will arise for the Jews from another place, but you and your father's house will perish. Yet who knows whether you have come to the kingdom for such a time as this?"

Esther responded, "Go, gather all the Jews who are present in Shushan, and fast for me; neither eat nor drink for three days, night or day. My maids and I will fast likewise. And so I will go to the king, which is against the law; and if I perish, I perish!"

She risked her life as she appeared unsummoned before the king to save her people. As a result of her selfless bravery, the people of Israel were not annihilated, and out of her lineage came the Messiah.

If I perish, I perish.

Later on that morning, a smile crept in as Katie and I stirred steaming bowls of oatmeal at her grandmother's kitchen table. We laughed and enjoyed the chance to be together in such an unexpected place and at such an unexpected time. My heart was still buzzing with dread and doubts, of course, but God had given me a fresh confidence for the day ahead.

With my hungry stomach filled and my body refreshed, I turned to the business of the day: finding Brian.

What a relief when the voice on the other end of the line wasn't his same old voice mail recording but his cheerful "Hello? Hello?" I nearly screamed when I heard it. "Brian!"

"Rifqa? Oh, my gosh! Where *are* you?"

"I waited all day at the church. Why didn't you come?"

"I *did* come. I couldn't find you. Where are you now?"

I told him about Katie and her mom, told him how I'd spent the night at her grandmother's house.

"Oh, thank goodness," he said. "I'm coming to get you *right now*. Don't go anywhere. Just tell me how to get there."

Relieved that my good friend hadn't abandoned me, I gave him the address and prepared again for a car ride that would drastically change my life.

As we waited in the living room for Brian to arrive, Katie's mom walked in with a polished black briefcase. She looked at me with a twinkle in her eye and said, "I have a few things for you." My body perked up with excitement at what it might be. "We need to figure out a way to make you blend in," she said with a wink in her voice. Then we all laughed when she pulled out a crazy-looking blond wig.

Laughter loosened the tense atmosphere as I modeled the wig in the living room mirror. Contrasted against my dark features, it looked ridiculous. It only succeeded in making me more noticeable than before.

"Maybe with these," I said with a mischievous tone, adding her pair of oversized seventies sunglasses to the ensemble. Howls continued to leap across the room. I tried them on with the wig and strutted across the living room with one hand on my hip, runway style. Forgoing the wig entirely, I reached for a navy blue Yankees baseball cap. Pulling back my dark hair into a messy bun, I scrunched my locks underneath the hat, pulling it down low to shield my face. Looking in the mirror, I chuckled at my reflection. My pretty green summer dress matched perfectly. I was going fashionably incognito.

It felt good in the moment to breathe again, to feel almost normal, not in a constant state of anxiousness. The rest of the morning, however, remained all too surreal, especially when Katie pulled the curtains open and said, "I think Brian's here." Running to the window, I saw his dark car pulling into the driveway. After praying for Katie's family and giving them all big hugs and "I love yous," I grabbed my backpack and ran out the door. Their crucial role in helping me escape would never be forgotten. I knew I hadn't thanked them properly, but it was all the time I could spare.

"Your kidnapper is here!" Brian said with a mischievous grin as I climbed inside. I responded with a fake "Ha, ha." Pulling away, I only had a moment to peer at Katie, standing at her front door. My heart ached to hold her close as I watched her weeping. We had both said goodbye in such a hurry, knowing the possibility of seeing each other again was slim. I reached my fingers to the car window, desiring to touch what I saw on the other side. Saying goodbye to her was like saying goodbye to a part of my childhood—my last physical tie to school, home, and more hopeful times. As I whispered a final "I love you, I'll miss you," we drove away. My heart twisted in pain at the thought of never seeing her again.

As we drove, Brian explained the plan to get me to Florida. Originally he was going to drive me all the way to the Lorenzes' house himself. But they had contacted some lawyers for advice on how best to keep me legally safe. They found out that if Brian drove me across state lines without my parents' permission, he could be charged with kidnapping a minor, even though I was the one asking for help.

In light of the legal recommendations, the Lorenzes decided the best plan of escape was for me to take a bus alone to Florida. One of their friends paid for my one-way ticket to Orlando. I was to pick up the ticket at the bus station in Columbus. Looking at the clock on Brian's dashboard, we realized we needed to race to get to the station before the bus took off without me.

Downtown traffic was slow and snarled as we squeezed past other cars and rushing pedestrians. The clock was ticking. The bus station wasn't easy to find, and once we did, we circled repeatedly, trying to find a close parking spot to reduce my chances of being seen. Pulling into the nearest one, we hopped out and sprinted toward the station. "It feels like we're in a movie," Brian said as we hustled along. "This is so crazy!" Once inside, we retrieved my bus ticket from the cashier and moved over to wait in the line for boarding.

So this was it.

It was time.

Brian said he wouldn't leave until I was safely on the bus. I wished he could come with me to protect me, but I knew that wasn't possible. I certainly didn't want him to get into legal trouble by coming with me on my escape.

As the line to board the bus shortened, he whispered to me sternly and seriously: "Rifqa, please do me a favor. Don't talk to anyone. Don't hug anyone. Don't pray for anyone. In fact, don't even *look* at anyone."

Barely able to handle my emotions, I smiled and nodded in tearful response to his fatherly passion for guarding me. I grabbed at his shirt, desperate to hold on to the only person who was safe. I couldn't let go. He could read me like a book.

With a big hug, he whispered, "Rifqa, God has you in His hands. You're going to be okay, all right? Heaven is cheering you on right now. You are not alone!"

Finally, I was next to board. The moment had come. I gave him one last hug and took a few steps forward. *How could I do this? Was it really going to work?* I set my foot on the stairway and looked back at him. Then—

I couldn't help it. I dodged out of line and ran back and hugged him again, a little longer this time. I knew the reason I was on my way to safety was because of this brave man's willingness not to cower away from helping me when it would've been so much easier to do nothing. I didn't know how I could possibly thank him. I would miss him so much.

The next time I stepped up on the bus stairs, I felt a strong hand touch my back—a powerful, mighty hand that I knew belonged to Jesus Himself. It gave me faith that no harm would befall me. And the entire time during the two-day bus trip, that hand never left.

The Greyhound coach was large, and even though it had seemed that a lot of people had been boarding, the spacious seating of the bus made it look relatively empty when I got inside. *Good.* The people on board were mostly African Americans who appeared to be in poverty. Holding on to the straps of my backpack, I slowly inched forward, feeling with every step the weight of the decision I was making, leaving everything behind. Eyeing the corner seat in the back, I sat down, glad for some solitude.

Things changed in a matter of minutes, however, when a group of obnoxious men clambered aboard and took over the back of the bus. One of them, a heavyset man, came and plopped down next to me. I wanted to get up and move, but I couldn't squeeze past him without asking *him* to move, and I didn't want to aggravate him. He kept repeating stories about how he had just been released from prison. He smelled like a sewer and continually cursed at no one in particular. I rolled my head back, mouthing to myself "unbelievable." His loud swearing was grating on my spirit, but I couldn't ask him to stop because Brian's words were echoing in my head: "Don't talk to anyone. Don't even *look* at anyone."

So I plugged my ears with my fingers, looked out the window, and clung to my backpack with both arms, hoping to be in my new home soon.

Eighteen

The two days on the bus were terrible. I didn't have any money or food or water, so I became significantly dehydrated. The bowl of oatmeal that Katie had served me was the only thing I'd eaten since before I left home, days before. I was deliriously weak and hungry. Starving.

About halfway into the journey, somewhere in Mississippi at one of our scheduled stops, I climbed off the bus just to give myself something to see and think about besides my empty stomach. What I saw, however, hardly made me feel any better. Uniformed policemen were circling and patrolling the area on foot.

Could they be looking for me? Already? My parents almost certainly would've called the police by now, so the idea of being traced through a bus ticket wasn't out of the realm of possibility. I lowered my Yankees cap to cover my face, hiding behind some larger passengers. Even my seat on the bus was a relief by the time I climbed aboard again to take off for the next leg of our trip. At least my foul-mouthed seatmate had gotten off.

Wrestling with anxiety and fatigue, I faded in and out of sleep—not quite awake, not quite all the way under—fertile soil for random scraps of memories that floated dream-like through my consciousness. At one point I could see my father holding up a large cream-colored sheet containing details of our family lineage: "One hundred fifty generations in our family, Rifqa, and every one of them has been Muslim!" He spoke it with such glimmering pride and honor while I pretended to be interested but couldn't have cared less. What a disappointment I knew I was being to him.

Another jostling of the bus, another memory dislodged. Back to the little Sri Lankan town where I was raised, where my father had held such leadership and influence. Back to the many hours I'd spent memorizing

the Qur'an and going to the mosque. Back to moments when I had tried
so hard to please and honor him, when all I ached for was to be held by
him, to hear him tell me he loved me no matter what, no matter who I
became, that I would always be his little girl. Yet every memory led me to
the same crushing truth. I'd never been capable of doing enough to satisfy
his pride. Love, in his eyes, was always conditional.

The words of a psalm I'd latched on to, ever since first reading it, now
filtered through my semi-wakeful state: "Father of the fatherless, a de-
fender of widows, is God in His holy habitation" (68:5).

I realized that the pain of my past might never go away, that I could
never completely outrun it or leave it in the rearview mirror. But I could
continue to press toward the One who had captured my heart. The God
of Abraham, Isaac, and Jacob promised a home to the broken, the lonely,
and the abandoned. I could feel His passion for me in that moment, burning warm within my spirit, drawing me forward across these endless miles
to freedom.

One by one the states rolled past my window: Kentucky, Mississippi,
Alabama, Georgia. At each of the twenty-five stops along the way, passengers got off and new ones got on—a constant rotation of diverse individuals. At one of the stops, a sweet black lady boarded who looked slovenly
and destitute, wearing an enormous pair of headphones. My heart was
moved toward this curious stranger. As she neared and settled into the seat
next to me, I flirted with the idea of striking up a conversation with her,
telling her about my faith in Christ. A few miles later, however, she suddenly cut loose in boisterous singing, belting out unashamedly, "I don't
care if I got nothing. I got Jesus. Oh, Hallelujah! Hallelujah!"

Why, I thought, had I judged her as being so needy of what I could
give to her? I needed what *she* had and was giving to *me*. I craved the selfless love of this woman who appeared to be utterly penniless and yet had
joy overflowing.

Humbled by the beauty of her raw, unbridled dependence on God, I felt a blanket of hope sweep around my wounded, weary shoulders as tears of repentance began to form and flow. Watching this woman made me want to trust Him like she did. She made me want to give up this sense of self-preservation that was driving me so fearfully to safety. I confessed to God that I knew I wasn't strong—I was weak physically and emotionally—and I needed Him to take care of me because I knew I couldn't do it myself. That evening, through the example of that woman, I rested my head on the window and willed myself to sleep, sure that my Father would protect and take care of me . . . sure that I belonged to Him.

It was late at night when I finally arrived. I'd been traveling for nearly two full days, embarking and disembarking, embarking and disembarking. But as I stepped off that bus for the final time, the warm Orlando air seemed to revive the little energy that remained in me. I had made it! Even though I'd never been to Florida, somehow it seemed like I was home.

As the door hissed shut behind me, I instantly heard an unfamiliar voice call out my secret name: "Anna! Over here!" Strangers who seemed to recognize me rushed up to greet me. Their smiles, their hugs, even now I still don't know how to adequately describe how reassuring and life-giving they truly were. I was here and I was safe. And I felt, oh, so loved.

They explained that, for security reasons, Blake and Beverly had sent them to pick me up at the station, that we'd be going to their house soon. "Are you hungry, Anna? We could stop and eat something first."

"Starving!" I said. I literally felt like it.

Any meal would've been heavenly to me that night, but this one was the most welcome and wonderful I could ever remember. The houses we passed as we left the restaurant and drove toward Blake and Beverly's were more upscale and grand than any I'd ever seen. It was so refreshing to be there, of course, and yet I could detect a competing emotion creeping in as well—this sense of feeling out of place in such a beautiful, unfamiliar area and social level. I began to doubt myself a little. *What if Beverly doesn't like me once she meets me and gets to know me?* She'd sounded so chirpy and cheerful on the phone. But as we pulled into their driveway, which led to another of these amazing homes, my thoughts wound me into a bit of a cocoon, making me feel a little timid.

I shouldn't have been. I'd no sooner stepped out of the car than an extremely tall man with kind eyes swooped me into a big bear hug. I guessed (I hoped) this was Blake.

"Hello, there!" he said, my baseball cap crushing under his embrace. "New York Yankees, huh? I *love* the Yankees. They're my favorite team."

Blake looked to be in his fifties. He had brown hair sprinkled with gray and a radiant smile.

And then, Beverly. I instantly recognized her from her Facebook photos. "Hello, sweet girl!" she said, squeezing me into another Lorenz hug. (Boy, did these guys ever love to show affection!) "You're so little!" she said, setting me at arm's length to get a better look. Her sparkling eyes and long brown hair delicately framed her face, complementing her youthful countenance. Yet she seemed to embody a depth and wisdom that shone deeply in her expression, the kind that's usually won only through hardship, the kind that belied her beautiful, glowing looks. I automatically connected with this pretty lady I'd never met before.

"It is so good to meet you! Welcome home!" she sang with her slight southern accent. I laughed to myself at how different an atmosphere this home and these people created compared with the one I'd come from. I wasn't sure I'd ever really believed that places like these actually existed.

Blake and Beverly's home seemed like a mini-mansion to me. I couldn't help but marvel at all the sparkly, delicate items and exquisite paintings that covered the walls and accented each room. It was quite a contrast to the empty walls and torn furniture in our little Ohio apartment. The only decorative object in our home was a dingy sign that said "Praise be to Allah" in Arabic.

I felt spoiled simply by being in these new surroundings, by being encouraged to make myself at home like family. I wanted to yelp with pure delight when they showed me my room. Amazing! It was painted a soothing pale green, with white curtains and elegant bedding. As much as I wanted to sit and visit with this dear family and find out everything I could possibly know about them—to experience the freedom of openly telling somebody the full, unvarnished story of my life—my body was drawn to the bed that looked so cozy and inviting after two days of being attached to a bus seat. I don't know how many hours I slept that night and into the next morning. But, my, did I feel refreshed when the new day dawned upon me. Feeling good. And feeling free.

The next two weeks floated by like a fairy tale. I almost didn't know how to live—free to do whatever I wanted, not being controlled by my family's culture, able to make decisions without needing to take into account how I could sneak around unnoticed. It felt like I was breathing for the first time in my life. Beverly took me on a shopping spree and bought brand-new clothes for me, just embracing me and loving me as if I were their own daughter. The acceptance and genuine tenderness I experienced in their home made me never want to leave.

If only life for me could truly be that simple.

On an otherwise average weekday, eight to ten hours from my family's home in Ohio, two detectives approached the receptionist's desk at a large nondenominational midwestern church and flashed their badges. Lennae, taken aback, asked what she could do to help them.

"Can you tell me if you've ever seen this girl?" the lead detective said, pulling a sheet of paper from the breast pocket of his jacket. With her brows furrowed in confusion, she examined the image of a young Asian girl with long, straight, dark hair and a blind right eye, seeming to be in her midteens.

"No sir, I haven't."

"Are you sure? She's a runaway who's been filed missing by her parents."

Lennae studied the paper again, wheeling through her memory banks to try placing the smiling girl from the picture. "I work here every day. I've never seen anyone who fits this description." They pressed her to see if they could speak with others, but no one else could attest to ever seeing me either.

Frustrated, having apparently reached the end of this particular trail, the officers looked back through their notes and asked a question that finally drew out a "yes" from Lennae as well as from the other staff members who'd emerged from their offices to see what the dramatic police-drama commotion was all about.

"Does a Brian Williams work here?"

Brian had been getting a barrage of calls from my father, who had somehow found his number and had left numerous threatening messages on his phone. Today, however, the calls had increased, not from my dad, but from government officials looking for information. Brian had done his best to dodge their questions, being cooperative without revealing my whereabouts. By nightfall he was trying to lay low, but he had a strong inner feeling that my secret was not going to hold.

When a sharp rapping on his apartment door jolted him from a dazed, shallow sleep, the adrenaline told him his time was probably up.

Two detectives pushed their way past him as he answered their knock, one of them pressing his badge toward Brian's face, the other beginning an immediate search of the home. "Brian Michael Williams," the first one said, "we have a pending warrant for your arrest. If Rifqa Bary does not show up in the next twenty-four hours, you're going to jail. Do you hear me, Mr. Williams?"

Meanwhile, in Orlando, I lay on a comfy couch and sipped southern sweet tea, watching the summer breeze blow gently against the trees outside the window. I'd been down here a couple of weeks, and while I knew I couldn't expect my parents to forget about me—pretend like everything was fine— the Lorenzes were working hard to keep me from being burdened by their worries and what was happening in the aftermath of my running away. They let me spend most of my days reading on the back porch or hanging out with them as a family. I was grateful to them for that.

But I couldn't help being curious. So in that settled moment, having grown a little more confident and acclimated to my new life by this time, I reached for my laptop, thinking I was ready to handle what I'd find. *No, wait—maybe I shouldn't.* My fingers retracted. But promising myself I wouldn't linger at whatever I found—just a quick, cursory check, nothing more—I started typing into the Google search bar: *Rifqa Ba—*

Boom!

"Rifqa Bary Missing" the first selection said. Clicking on the headline, I read the feature story's subhead. "After Nearly 2 Weeks, New Albany Teen Still Missing." And I saw the image of my freshman school picture. I clutched my hand to my mouth. I was *all over* the news! Scrolling down, I even came across a Facebook page announcing that my school was gathering to remember me through a "balloon-letting-go ceremony."

"This is crazy!" I uttered, setting my tea on the table. My disappearance was obviously a much bigger deal than I imagined it would be.

Something felt comforting about being missed and cared for, honestly, but I also felt saddened that no one had known what had been going on in my home all that time.

I felt good and I felt bad.

I felt scared.

Blake asked if I'd like to run some errands with him downtown. Our driving path took us by a large imposing structure among the other buildings that made up the urban sector of Orlando. "What's that place?" I asked.

"That? Oh, it's the Orange County Juvenile Detention Center."

And almost without skipping a beat, this obscure thought strode cruelly through my mind: *One day you're going to be there.*

Nineteen

I t was dinner time, and Rosa's husband, the expert in gourmet Cuban cooking, called the family to the kitchen. All four children filed in, with Rosa following, just as the phone rang. She quickly escaped the kitchen before her husband could give her that look that says no business calls at the dinner table.

"Hello?"

"Hi, is this Rosa Armesto? My name is Blake Lorenz. Your name and number were given to me by members of my church. They told me that you do pro bono work for the Christian attorneys' organization Alliance Defending Freedom. I was hoping you could help us. My wife and I are pastors. We have given refuge in our home to a sixteen-year-old girl who's afraid for her life. Her Muslim father has threatened to kill her for converting to Christianity. We need legal help because she is filed missing in Columbus, Ohio, as a runaway."

The story moved Rosa's maternal heart. *Poor girl! And only sixteen . . .* She thought of her own daughter who was only a few years away from that age.

Blake was right. *Not too many people would be willing to touch my case, and even fewer would possess expertise in this highly complicated aspect of the law.*

Rosa's caseload and calendar screamed at her not to do it. She was already doing too much, missing the kids much more than she liked. Plus, she was in Miami, and this was all happening in Orlando. There were a lot of reasons for saying no.

She said yes, she'd think about it.

Unbeknownst to Blake, Rosa had experience in child dependency and juvenile delinquency. These were two unique areas of the law, and she knew exactly what needed to be done.

Later that evening Rosa shared with her brother about the new case.

His response was definitely not exuberant. "Can't they find another lawyer? Why you? I am just concerned that taking on this case will bring serious repercussions from your employer . . . I am not so sure about this, Rosa."

Those same doubts and thoughts lingered in her mind when she asked the Lorenzes the same question.

"Why me? Are there other attorneys that you can find to take on this case, maybe closer to Orlando? It may be a lot simpler for you . . ."

Beverly and Blake sighed with exhaustion. How could they possibly convey all the effort they had put into searching for someone, anyone who would take the case?

"Oh, Rosa, we've called over ten attorneys all over the country. Some of whom are prestigious and well known for their work. Yet the few who said they'd do it, they just don't have understanding and experience in child dependency. All the others declined, mostly because of the religious sensitivity, I think. You're the only one we've found that we believe can represent Rifqa strongly. We have tried, Rosa, but there is no one else that can help. Please help us."

She still had reservations. She still felt conflicted about it. Yet something in her made her yearn to do everything in her power to help fight for freedom. For justice.

Rosa was in.

I'll never know how much time Blake and Beverly spent researching the validity of my perceived threat and the avenues they could walk down in trying to keep me safe. They weren't lawyers, just concerned believers brave enough to step in where others wouldn't. Although many people, hearing my sad tale, would've been quick to pass me off as a scared girl jumping to wild conclusions, the Lorenzes listened without closing their minds to the possibility that I might actually be telling the truth.

Blake handed me a newspaper article with the headline "Honor Killing in America." It was the story of a young girl in Texas who, along with her sister, had been shot and killed by their father in the back of his taxicab because they'd become too Westernized, taking non-Muslim boyfriends. Googling the account later, I discovered it to be just the tip of a tragic iceberg: fathers killing daughters and brothers killing sisters. Most of the reports involved childhood offenses equally as minor as the girls' actions in Texas—manner of dress, choice of friends—nothing compared to my own renouncing of Islam and embracing of Christianity, dishonoring both faith and family. Yet the blood of all these girls testified to the reality of my experience.

I honestly hadn't heard these reports before. I just knew I hadn't imagined or exaggerated what had happened in my home. It was horrible. It was abusive. It was real. And the more I read, the more it made sense. I was even more convinced that my parents and their mosque meant business when they said they'd "take care" of me.

Although I had been abused most of my life, I had lived in denial for a long time. I guess no one instantly recognizes what's abnormal about her home life when it's always been her normal. As I'd become older, increasingly pained and aware that my experience shouldn't be happening, I was terrified by the possibility of making it worse by telling my friends the true danger I felt I was in. That's why I'd gone ahead with the deception, once Christ's jealousy for my soul had proven too much for me to fend off. That's why I'd been willing to cope with smuggling a Bible into the bathroom, for example, and now even running to total strangers nearly half a country away. Why would I have done that simply to avoid being grounded or being punished or losing some of the cherished privileges of adolescence? No, I'd been warned in private, and I would've been dispatched in private, long before anyone with reasonable care and concern could've come to my rescue. Blake and Beverly knew that. Brian had known that. And they each had put themselves at great risk to make sure it never came to that.

But sometimes there's only so much you can do, even when you're trying to do the right thing.

Not too many days later, I was enjoying a normal night in the Lorenz household, watching a Disney movie with their two grown daughters, Elizabeth and Suzanna. Their parents had gone to bed early, and I was eating up the chance to just laugh and relax. All the joy faded, however, when Blake could suddenly be heard coming down the hall, nearing the room we were in. His voice had that sound. Tense. Something was wrong. I could just tell.

He staggered in, half-asleep, talking on his cell phone, wearing a T-shirt and pajama bottoms. Beverly trailed behind him, looking exhausted and concerned.

"Did you tell them where she is?" Blake asked the caller.

I pretended not to overhear, but I was obviously the subject. Everyone was trying to make out who was calling and what was being said, based on the snippets we could hear from Blake's side of the conversation. Covering the mouthpiece with his hand, Blake whispered, "The police are after Brian. They want to arrest him if Rifqa doesn't show up."

My face went pale. My heart dropped. I felt so guilty. I couldn't bear the thought. Brian imprisoned? Because of *me*? I couldn't let it happen. Blake rubbed his forehead with his palm and continued listening to Brian explain what had happened.

Elizabeth turned to me and said assertively, "Rifqa, go upstairs." I gladly obeyed. I didn't want to hear any more than I already had.

I furiously paced across my dark bedroom, back and forth, waving my hands in the air, silently mouthing my prayers. For fifteen minutes or more I wrestled again with the all-too-familiar worry I'd been spared from these

past two glorious weeks. Blake and Beverly's nervous voices continued fil-
tering upstairs, while shards of reality crashed through the dome of safety
and security I'd recklessly tried to build for myself. I couldn't let this happen to Brian—and I wouldn't. I would be the one to take responsibility for
my actions.

I would turn myself in.

It was the right thing to do.

Gliding slowly downstairs, dreading each measured step and where it
was taking me, I found Blake sitting at the kitchen table, staring blankly
into the distance, the disengaged phone still in his hand. In the grave silence of that moment and the harsh brightness of the kitchen lights, he
looked as though he'd aged years in a matter of weeks. My presence in their
home had undoubtedly been more stressful than I'd wanted to believe.

"Let's call the police and tell them where I am," I said. I meant it to
sound bold and resolute. It was tinged mostly with fear instead.

Blake's face grew solemn at my statement. He knew, because I was a
minor, that he and Beverly were technically harboring a runaway. They'd
consulted with numerous attorneys and politicians, and all agreed that
according to both state and federal law, they could legitimately be charged
with a serious crime. In one way it didn't make sense. Justice seemed to cry
out that *something* could be done to help a person in my life-threatening
situation. This couple should be hailed as heroes rather than hounded as
felons, but the law was moving swiftly, without waiting to listen to all the
pertinent details. This dear man who'd become my precious friend knew
I was giving him the only answer that either of us could accept.

"All right," he replied huskily, once again rubbing his forehand with
his palm. I pulled one of the kitchen chairs forward and quietly sat down
next to him, clutching my Bible in hand.

As he found and dialed the number to the missing children hotline,
I started to quietly whisper the words of Psalm 91—"He who dwells in
the secret place of the Most High shall abide under the shadow of the

Almighty"—attempting to relieve the insulting stress of being put on hold while making such a life-defining phone call. Not to mention, the cheerful on-hold music was a disgrace to the sober moment. The trumpet on the phone blared joyfully as I tried to be confident in what God's Word said. Finally someone answered and transferred Blake to someone else. Then someone else. The irony of meeting such stiff bureaucratic resistance for attempting to report an active police matter was, well, surprising.

"I will say of the LORD, 'He is my refuge and my fortress; my God, in Him I will trust.'" I kept repeating the same passage over and over again, hoping to find some relief from the agony I felt.

Once the deed was done—officially reporting that an underage runaway was under his roof—we fully expected blue lights to begin circling the driveway at any minute. That's how they're supposed to react to a call like this, isn't it?

But no one came. No one called back. No one kicked open the doors to take me away.

Nothing.

Days passed, and still no one showed up. The lack of response from the authorities almost felt worse than if they'd come to get me right away. Each day prolonged the angst of what the future would hold. The not knowing, the not being able to psyche myself up and adequately prepare—it was slow torture. We fought to mask the anxiety by trying to keep the atmosphere light. Yet everybody in the house was nervous and scared. They tried hard to be strong and upbeat, but their sleep-deprived, soul-dismayed eyes revealed a different story.

I often pushed away the sorrow by cleaning. As I wiped the railings of the stairwell, I could concentrate on a mindless household task rather than allow myself to float off in unfettered worry. I felt better staying close to home, where I wasn't expected to be anything other than pressured and preoccupied, and yet where my usually cheerful, beaming smile could stand out against the grieving thoughts and expressions of the family. But if my demeanor ever fooled them, I knew it couldn't fool God. I was in agony, needing something to happen if something was *going* to happen. My soul languished for lasting freedom and safety.

Four days later the doorbell rang. Before any of us could barely register the sound or come anywhere close to reaching the door, a sturdy knock immediately followed. The urgency drew all our eyes in that direction, yet we all seemed simultaneously frozen by fear. Beverly's voice shook as she cried, "Blake!"

He came out of their bedroom and boldly moved forward to meet our visitor.

Before Blake opened the door, I instinctively sprinted up the stairs with my adrenaline running strong. Peeking through the railing, I strained to see an Orange County sheriff's deputy standing in the entry. I didn't need to hear the conversation to know why he was here.

"I'm here to investigate a report of a missing runaway," he stated, looking at a piece of paper. I wished I could be invisible and blend into the background, holding on tightly enough to avoid being taken.

"Well, she is obviously here," I heard Blake answer, motioning his head upstairs to where I was lying flat and motionless on the beige carpet but not doing a good job of hiding. Breathing in courage, I made my way downstairs. I had come this far. Time to go through with it.

I shared my story as best I could, and the officer listened silently. He looked to be in his early forties and was peaceful in the way he carried himself. He frequently nodded as I spoke. It seemed to me, as outrageous as all of it probably sounded, that he believed me. But after hearing me out, he looked at me and gently said, "I'm sorry, but I still have to follow the rules and take you away. This is protocol. I'm so sorry." His words were hard to swallow, but his soft voice made me feel safe. Grieving, I nodded with understanding.

They'd gotten me.

It was an extremely hot day even by Florida standards. My mocha-colored skin baked under the direct sunlight as I stepped out of the Lorenzes' house, walking barefoot and grabbing my sandals in one hand. Clutching my Bible for security in the other hand, I inched forward down the walk, with Beverly's arm around my shoulders the entire way. As we arrived at the sheriff's car in front of the driveway, Beverly sighed, squeezed me hard, and grudgingly let go. With a long gaze, I soaked in her comforting presence for as long as I could, then turned away, defeated, broken. I let out a sorrowful moan, more from the ache in my heart than from the pain in my burning feet. Through clenched teeth, I whispered my final goodbyes to the rest of my family.

And I was gone.

I couldn't help but peer out the back window as we pulled away. Craning my neck, I could see Blake's arms around Beverly, comforting her as she wept. I had never seen her cry the entire time I was there; she was a strong woman. Soon their image through the window grew smaller and smaller until they were only a dot in a distance.

My only comfort now was my Bible, which the officer had allowed me to bring. I didn't need to wonder long where he was taking me.

Twenty

The deputy's car rolled to a stop next to the Orange County Juvenile Detention Center, the place I'd felt the premonition about just a week or so earlier. He turned around in the front seat and said, "I'm so sorry, but I'll need to come around and handcuff you now. I really don't want to do this to you, but [those words again] it's protocol." He exited the car, opened my door, and to his open discomfort, he handcuffed me.

"Uh . . . ," I said as I slipped my hands out of the cuffs.

He smiled and produced a pair of smaller handcuffs designed for children, tightening them to my petite size, binding my wrists together. The kind look on his face somehow soothed me a little. If I was being forced into going to jail, I'm sure the arresting officer's ordeal could've been a whole lot worse. With the sound of the cuffs locking my wrists, he led me forward.

But jail. Why? I felt I had done nothing wrong. I had run away from home because my life was in danger for believing in Jesus Christ. Why was that such a horrendous crime? Why was *I* the one in trouble? The only explanation the deputy could give me was that runaways were taken to jail to keep them from running away again, securing them in lockdown. But I was perfectly content in the place I'd chosen to live with the Lorenzes. The only place I wanted to run away from now was this place.

The smell, the people, the sounds, the language—everything was a nightmare. My rights as a human being seemed to vanish. I was only allowed to breathe and move within a certain area. If I were ever to leave that area, I would be reprimanded. So for hours I did the only two things I was able to do: sit and pray. And I continually asked the officials, "Sir, Ma'am, are you going to send me back to Ohio?" Each time, their response was emotionless and silent.

Why? Why were they doing this? Treating me like a criminal?

Someone finally came in and shoved an ugly navy jumpsuit in my direction. In trade, I was forced to give up everything else I had—the clothes on my back, my precious Bible the deputy had allowed me to bring, even the hair tie that held my hair out of my face. They said it was part of the suicide prevention procedure. Then they stood me in front of a camera, forced my hands into ink so they could raise fingerprints, and took mug shots. For the first time in my life, I didn't smile for the camera.

It only got worse. I was told, because I'd been reported as a missing runaway, they were required by law to contact my parents and inform them of my whereabouts. I'd need to sit there and listen while they rang the number and talked with them on speaker phone. "Right this way . . ."

I was led into a pale yellow room. Soon my father's voice was echoing off the walls and raining down on my head like the sound of a ghost, haunting me from my past. I hated, *hated* hearing it. Fear, anger, hurt, adrenaline. I felt assaulted by more emotions than I could handle all at once.

"Can I please speak to my daughter?" he said.

No, I shook my head violently, gritting my teeth in abject refusal. I knew exactly how this scene would go, and I wasn't about to be made to look like the problem here. He was going to lure me back by convincing the authorities that he was safe, that he was sorry, that I was overreacting and misinformed. My father's a salesman; he's a master at convincing people. Most people who meet him for the first time think he is a kind man. His gentle eyes, bright smile, and exotic accent give the impression of a loving father. Yet no one knew what kind of a man he was, the man he so quickly and frequently became in the confines of our Muslim home. His facade infuriated me, hearing it masqueraded again in this creepy place where I was chained down and forced to listen to it.

"Rifqa," he said, "please come back home. I don't know where you have gotten this nonsense. You can practice Christianity."

Liar. I knew all too well the truth. His threats were too fresh in my mind for me to believe him for a minute. Disgust enveloped me. I knew it was all a show for the authorities. He wanted it to look like I was lying. I shook my head in disagreement, staying silent, then finally whispered quietly but firmly to the officials in the room, *"No, I don't want to talk to him."* They couldn't make me.

Finally it was over. Let them think what they want to think. *I* knew the truth. If there was any hope of justice, the truth would ultimately come out. No one can do what my father had done repeatedly, repeatedly, repeatedly to me and then get away with it. Can they? *Can they?*

That's what Rosa Armesto was going to find out when she called the detention center shortly thereafter and demanded to speak with me. I had never met her, had only spoken with her once on the phone, and didn't know for sure that she'd agreed to take on my case pro bono. Legally, she was the only person I was able to talk to, and her mothering voice was sweet to my ears, especially after the outrage of my father's call.

"Honey, just tell them the entire story," she calmly advised.

Her words broke me into tears. Any strength I'd displayed so far was suddenly depleted at the recognition that this whole thing could go horribly wrong, that it was just me and my story against whatever my father's wily manipulation could spin against me. In that moment I'm sure I looked the part of a terrified sixteen-year-old girl who'd never imagined in her wildest dreams that she'd be hauled off like a criminal and placed behind bars.

What were these people going to do to me?

At some point—I suppose as a survival mechanism God created for the human body—no situation has the power to keep us at unbearable heights of emotion forever. Even the gritty, degrading, fully exposed trauma of being in such a horrible place as jail finally settles into a reality that you can only accept, even temporarily. Tears finally run out. Sensitivities adapt. Shock values diminish over time.

As I sat in the holding area, waiting to be moved to an actual cell, I could sense the Spirit of God rising up again in my spirit—through the dimming emotions of my father's phone call, through the more predictable movements of the staff and surroundings around me—wooing me to trust Him, to believe in Him, to surrender my weak grip on sanity into His everlasting arms of love and wisdom. To be willing to experience what He means when He says His strength is made for human weakness.

With a deep sigh of surrender, I decided to make the most of whatever time I was assigned to spend there. I would be His vessel, giving off whatever amount of light He could generate through one so frightened and fragile. I felt like Psalm 27:6 coming to life: "And now my head shall be lifted up above my enemies all around me; therefore I will offer sacrifices of joy in His tabernacle; I will sing, yes, I will sing praises to the LORD." Against all reason, I was going to sit tall, hold my head up, and smile. I was going to emit the peace and joy that God had fashioned inside my heart. Since this was where my journey to freedom had led me—jailed confinement—I would declare my freedom nonetheless.

One officer, passing by throughout that long seven or eight hours of waiting, said, "Do you know where you are? You're in *jail,* honey." And he laughed. Yet I answered his cruel laughter with a nodding smile. They could do whatever they wanted to do to me; I would keep whispering to myself the name of Jesus and hope that in their long, confused stares they were sensing His presence as well.

Finally, my name was called.

My room, apparently, was ready for me.

What I discovered, however, was that this downtown building was some sort of clearinghouse, a switching station, the central hub where minors under arrest could be brought for booking. From there, criminals were shipped to outlying facilities where they'd pay their debt to society.

So as my coach and departure time arrived, they secured my hands with a chain that attached to my legs and waist, preventing any attempt on my part at making a fast getaway. My chains were then chained to another guy's, who was taking the long van ride along with me. His dark-chocolate face bore all the weight of the oppression he was under, for whatever he'd done that had landed him in this place. I looked into his bloodshot eyes and felt compassion for him, even as we were herded with the others like animals into a cage, dragging our heavy metal chains, directed into the wagon by a guard with a baton.

Forty-five minutes later we reached our destination, and the waiting commenced again. The boys went one way; the girls went the other. And the hours slowly trickled away in a place where time stands still and waits for paperwork.

Finally, after a long round of questioning (which at least made the time pass more quickly), I was ordered into a shower room where the indignities could really begin. I was told to strip naked, forced to submit to a total body search (checking for hidden drugs or weapons), then allowed a timed two-minute shower in freezing, ice-cold water. I was starting to fully realize the culture of imprisonment: utter humiliation. The shockingly cold water beat down hard against my bare skin as I closed my eyes and prayed to endure it.

The whole atmosphere was brutal. Bright, hot lights shone down harshly on the hallways as they led me to my cell, commanding me to walk with my hands behind my back or else face their discipline. The cells were . . . ohhh . . . awful. How I missed my lovely pale-green room at the Lorenzes. This one was small and gray, looking more like a dungeon than sleeping quarters. A thin padding of mattress lay over a concrete cot, across from a sink and an open, dirty toilet with an overpowering stench. A small window to the outside world was cut into the wall above me, but it was much too high to actually see out of. A drinking fountain, if you wanted to call it that, was in the corner. The whole basin as well as the wall behind it was covered in green algae. Disgusting.

I could not understand how what I had done merited this treatment.

The first night was so frightening that I don't remember sleeping much at all. The bright lights blazed all night long, and the chilly temperatures felt like someone was breathing frosty air onto my body the whole time. Lying on the cement bed, I huddled into a tiny ball to try to stay warm, burying my face against my knees, away from the light and the biting air. And then just as I finally started to doze off, a blood-curdling scream, coming from somewhere outside my cell, jarred me to full attention.

I was shivering on my feet before I even realized I was up. *What's happening? What's going on?* I peeked through the little window that looked out over the hallway to see what all the commotion was about. I spied a young black girl tied down to her bed in the middle of the hall. She was growling and biting at the metal chains with her teeth. My heart grieved for her just as I grieved for myself. I fought through the horror of it as best I could, crawling back onto my stony bed and trying to fall asleep while the girl's anguished cries pierced the air. I slept that night crying harder than I ever had. I could hear the sound of my own sobs echoing in my cell.

When I awoke again—still night—my throat felt desperately parched. What I wouldn't give for a drink of water, except I wouldn't dare touch my lips to anything that spewed from that rancid fountain. Tapping on my door to try getting the guard's attention, I asked the sweet-looking lady who approached if she (please) could perhaps give me a drink of water.

"I'm sorry," she said disappointedly, understandingly. "I can't open the door at night. If you want water, you'll have to drink from the fountain."

Ugh. Okay. (No way.)

"But by the way," she said, "read Romans 8."

Romans 8? Oh yeah! I recognized her now. She was the woman whom, at some point in this impossibly long day and night, I'd told how they'd taken my Bible from me and asked if she could get it for me or give me one. I smiled at her now through my tiny peephole of access to human contact and thanked her. She had warmed my cold, stony heart.

Balling up again on my bed, I opened the Bible she'd given me and read from the passage she'd suggested: "What then shall we say to these things? If God is for us, who can be against us? He who did not spare His own Son, but delivered Him up for us all, how shall He not with Him also freely give us all things? Who shall bring a charge against God's elect? It is God who justifies." Again, like so many times before and yet perhaps never as perceptibly as now, His Word came crashing through the iron bars of fierce opposition, undeterred by any stubborn obstacle in its way, and said hello to His child who could never be kept from His care and attention.

I was able to sleep till morning on the pillow of His grace.

For the next few days and nights, life in jail became my new normal. We were ushered into the cafeteria to eat terrible food in silence, then ushered back to spend lonely days in a six-by-eight container. A few days on the outside can fly past and we wonder where the week's gone; a few days in jail feels like it's never going to end. The only thing that lay out there on the horizon for me was a court hearing with the judge, where I hoped I could say something to somebody to explain what had happened and maybe get an explanation for why my actions were worthy of these consequences.

Maybe, hopefully, I could get out of here.

Twenty-One

I*t's time for court!"* the booming voice at my door announced, the guard banging on my cell. Every noise in this place made me jump, made me scared.

Going to court. I didn't know what to expect. The idea felt terribly foreboding as I did what little I was able to do to get ready and then walked out of my cell under guarded escort. I realized this action represented a potential hint of forward progress in my case, but the unknown spiked anxiety in me. My heart felt like lead.

As they congregated us—those with hearings scheduled for the day—together, I recognized the dark, ghostly countenance of the boy I'd been chained alongside on the van ride to this place. He, like all of us—even me, I guess—looked like a hopeless criminal. So much for the "innocent until proven guilty" philosophy. There's something about a prison jump-suit that equalizes the playing field and passes sentence without saying a word. But like before, I was intent on my public face being as bright and unaffected as I could make it. So as I approached the group, I smiled at one of the guards and chirped, "Good morning!"

"Humph!" he snorted, mocking me. "You look so happy to be in jail. *Bless your heart,*" he smarted off sarcastically while attaching heavy chains to my hands, waist, and feet as before, then linked me to the parade of other juveniles. I was pretty sure the chains outweighed my body weight of seventy-five pounds, so walking was a chore. But sucking in my breath and dragging my chains behind me, I kept telling myself, *What an honor, Rifqa, to be suffering for Christ, walking in the footsteps of your Lord.*

The rear area of the white van was pitch black. Thick, dark veils on the windows blocked every inch of sunlight, completely cutting off any contact with the outside world. Not until we'd idled in place for the longest time did my eyes adjust enough to the darkness that I could see little pinholes of light around the edges. Through one of them, from where I was seated, I could almost make out the colors of a hot pink flower blooming outside. That's what I hoped to be like: a ray of unabashed joy and promise, shining in a place where darkness and hopelessness claimed such a monopoly on everyone's emotions. I shouldn't be here, but God had not forsaken me. I prayed I wouldn't forsake Him either.

"This way!" the guard demanded once we arrived at the courthouse building and were shuffled inside. Having seen nothing but the dreariness of a jail interior for so long, I was a little enlivened by the relative beauty of the courtroom: polished benches, leather chairs, glossy caramel-colored desks. Everything looked grand. Even the audience as well as the staffers and other legal personnel in suits and ties and pencil skirts stood out in sharp, attractive contrast to my grubby navy-blue prison uniform, my thick metal chains, and my wildly unkempt hair.

As I looked around, my heart nearly leaped out of my chest when I recognized a familiar face. *Beverly!* I would've done anything in that moment to feel her embrace. Upon seeing me, she waved hesitantly then started shaking and silently sobbing. Her reaction confirmed what I didn't want to admit: I looked as dreadful on the outside as I felt on the inside.

The call to order interrupted this thought as the day's docket began. The purpose of these hearings, as I understood it, was for us to be officially read what we had been charged with and to give us a brief opportunity to respond to the judge with various questions and claims of rebuttal. The judge could then decide how our individual cases would proceed. So one by one, my fellow inmates stepped forward as their names were called. I prayed for each of them as I waited my turn, listening to the various reasons why each was in chains. One story in particular made my heart ache. A tall young man stood before the judge, who ruled in this case that she was releasing him from custody. But his mother then stood to speak, ask-

ing the court to keep him in jail because she couldn't handle him. Her son
reacted to her plea by breaking into deep, wailing sobs.

It was enough to make me physically sick. And yet it was only one of
many. Person after person, boys and girls, paraded before the judge, each
of their stories so sad and unfortunate.

And then it was my turn.

Blake stood from his seat and approached the bench with me, holding
me in a big hug and helping me forward. When I was invited to speak, I
tried to sound stronger than I felt.

"Your Honor . . ." But before I could finish my sentence, my voice
broke with emotion. "Will I have to go back to Ohio? Please don't send me
back. Please! I'm so scared! Please!"

Blake squeezed me to comfort me and told the judge that my attorney
would be appearing by phone. He had given Rosa's number to the court
clerk. We could hear Rosa on the speaker phone explaining that I was
threatened by my parents and requesting that I be placed in the custody of
the Department of Children and Families. Thankfully, the judge agreed,
temporarily, but it wasn't over.

"It's time for school!" Back at the jail, it was always time for something
you didn't want to do. Court yesterday, school today. By school, it wasn't
like a teacher leading students from the front of the room in some kind of
coursework. An observer silently monitored us from the corner, but otherwise it was a large room with desks where kids read or wrote, working by
themselves or just not doing anything, just being there, a break from soli-
tary confinement. I read my Bible, off by myself, turning the pages with
cuffed hands that made everything difficult and made me miss my freedom at every moment.

The classroom was as gray and dreary as everything else in the building. It wasn't like the preppy atmosphere of New Albany High, that was

for sure. Out of the corner of my eye, I glanced at the other girls in the room; they all looked much younger than I. Soon a handful of them approached and asked, "Why are *you* here?"

Well, that's a long story, obviously. But the more I shared, the more they seemed eager to hear. So I told them how God had changed my life, and how I'd been forced to run away from my family as a result. I told them that following Jesus wasn't just a good idea to me, but that He was the One I lived for. Soon others were turning their heads and looking, listening. One or two of them screeched their desks toward me until I was almost encircled. Even the officers were looking my way, and not just to see if we were planning an escape. One of the girls cried, tears of regret and remembrance seeming to mingle with her tears of need and hope. Passion burned in my bones as I told them who Jesus is. I felt valiant in that moment. I was more convinced than ever that I'd done the right thing by running away from home.

Later that afternoon, still glowing with fresh zeal for God while sitting alone again in my cell, I sensed what had become for me an almost absolute assurance of His presence: a gentle whisper that resonated in my spirit and spoke to me with a simple knowing.

Will you sing to Me, Rifqa? the whisper seemed to ask.

Sing to You? Here? Are You serious? I'm sitting in a jail cell. They'll think I'm crazy. A song? I don't even know if I remember any!

I don't know how long I wrestled with God. I had no access to a clock, so there was never any way to determine how much time passed, not just then but at *any* point during my time in jail. Yet I knew He would win in the end. He always does. I couldn't help but cave in to His love. I embraced what He was telling me, embraced all the pain of my life in that dreadful, interminable place, and prayed, *Okay, God. Give me a song to sing and I'll sing it.*

I softly rested the back of my head against the wall, exhaled a cleansing sigh, swallowed my last remnant of hindered, self-conscious disobedience, and began singing the opening lines to Matt Redman's "The Heart of Worship"—the only song that came into my head.

I sang every word, every verse. And then, since I'd followed Him this far, I repeated the last line over and over: *"It's all about You. It's all about You, Jesus."* This simple song became my prayer. A sense of His presence flooded every pore in my body, much the same way His love had transfused into my being on that Friday night all those years ago in Angela's church sanctuary. I began weeping for joy. I could sense God's nearness, knowing He was so proud of me. I could feel His deep affection and delight over my life.

And finally, I just couldn't take it anymore, couldn't hold it all in. My voice echoed loudly within the confined walls of my cell, as I lifted my face toward the ceiling and cried out with the fullness of my worshipful heart, *"I love You, Jesus!"*

"You are worth it, Lord," I prayed aloud. "I'll stay here for the next twenty years if I have to. I can't live without Your presence, God! I'll do *anything*! I'll go *anywhere* if You're with me!" I felt like I was gazing straight into heaven. Hunger for Him and loyalty to Him became my obsession from the inside out. It didn't matter that I was chained wrongly for a crime I never committed. My spirit soared with hope. I surrendered my life to God again. Everything seemed to make sense in that moment—or at least I was fully confident that it made perfect sense to Him. If I were sent back to Ohio into the hands of my parents, it didn't matter anymore. If I were beaten or hurt, it didn't matter anymore. If I were flown back to Sri Lanka or even killed at the hands of my father, it didn't matter anymore. Jesus was enough. Life or death, I would follow Him. And I didn't care who knew it.

Meanwhile, in Miami, my attorney Rosa was fighting like a lioness. Beverly had called her, hysterical, after seeing me in court, observing me in my jail clothes. "Please get our girl out of there, Rosa," she begged. Beverly is normally the confident and assertive type, but seeing me chained like an animal had nearly killed her spirit. She hadn't been able to eat or sleep.

"Beverly, I am going to do everything I can. We *will* get her out."

Rosa did her magic. She worked her connections and got to the right people until she'd made her point in no uncertain terms: this girl, her client, was in danger. And if the state even *considered* sending me back to Ohio without taking seriously my testimony, my blood would be on Florida's hands. Furthermore, she said, I had done nothing wrong; I had only acted in self-defense, and I represented no kind of flight risk because I didn't want to leave here. I had come here on my own initiative. By rights, I should be out of that jail before the sun went down *tonight*!

And I was.

A few hours later, the day before my seventeenth birthday, an officer opened my cell door and said, "You're released." Surely I was dreaming. Or surely she was joking. But she wasn't. I followed her through a winding maze of corridors until I finally saw the outside world gleaming through the glass doors—and Blake standing in the glow of it. I ran and hugged him, wrapping my arms around him and squeezing him as if he might disappear should I ever let go.

I wasn't dreaming. I was free!

"We have temporary custody over you until tomorrow, Rifqa, when the hearing resumes," Blake said as the officer handed me a bag containing my clothes and my few belongings, then pointed to a closed cell and motioned for me to go in and change. After putting on my own clothes, I sighed with comfort. It felt so good to wear a pretty dress again.

When I returned to where Blake was waiting, I was wearing sandals and staring at my pretty manicured toenails, painted pink. The polish hadn't completely worn off from Beverly's and my girl-time outing when we'd both gotten our nails done, now a week ago.

Pink. Like the pink flower I'd seen from the prison van. I hoped the joy in me wouldn't fade before the coming trouble was over.

Twenty-Two

Rosa, Blake, Beverly, and I went to dinner that evening. No more jail food. No more jail *anything*. But there was plenty of talk about legal things, and I tried my best to grasp and process the intricacies of what Rosa was trying to explain.

"It's a very sensitive case," she said, "because the pendulum could swing one of two ways: either as a criminal case—an underage girl running away from home and her parents filing charges against her. Or as a dependency case—based on allegations of abuse against her family. We need to get DCF (the Florida Department of Children and Families) involved in order to keep her in the state under state custody. But as of now, they're trying to spin it as Rifqa being a runaway, viewing it as criminal activity. If they're successful, they can legally send her back to Ohio into the hands of her family members. We'll be powerless to do anything."

I was mortified to hear that. So they could still send me home? Even though the judge had said no?

"But if there are abuse allegations—which there are—we can request for DCF to investigate the case. That way the state of Florida will be her guardian, and the case will stay in Orlando. They won't be able to send her back."

This sounded more hopeful. But still . . .

Beverly's forehead wrinkled with concern. "But what about her legal status? Even if we're able to keep her in Florida, she could be deported because she has no paperwork."

Rosa's face lightened a little as she leaned toward Beverly, resting a hand on hers for comfort. "Here's the providence of God in all of this, and why I'm so glad you called me. Having worked in dependency, I know some things about this whole area of the law that most attorneys, even some immigration attorneys, don't know. There is something called 'special immigrant juvenile status' that allows underage children without legal immigration status—who are a dependent of the state—to apply for a green card so they can stay in the country legally. If we can convince the judge to accept Rifqa's case as a dependency case, we can file for special immigrant juvenile status, and her immigration issue can be resolved."

I let her words sink in. So there was no in-between. It basically came down to whichever way we could get the court to consider the case. One was a total loss; the other at least gave me hope of protection. Rosa's eyes spoke volumes of how sobering the situation was. Either decision from the judge would change my life dramatically.

It was hard to be *too* distressed, however. I'd be sleeping at the Lorenzes tonight, with a clear glass of water by my bedside and a clean bathroom just down the hall. Not to mention, the next day would be my seventeenth birthday, even if it would need to double as a hearing day.

Oh, what a Monday it would turn out to be.

I woke up that morning feeling the taste of freedom. Elizabeth Lorenz had given me a beautiful laced white dress as a birthday gift, and I decided to wear it immediately on what I hoped would be a day of total victory. I walked from the car holding on to Blake's arm, breathing the fresh air, and feeling his strength next to me. I tried to convince myself that everything was going to be okay.

But—first surprise of the day—my case had been delayed. Likely until the afternoon. We'd need to wait and see. When dealing with the courts, I discovered it's best to expect the unexpected.

Then—surprise number two—as we were leaving the courthouse, I happened to spot him. *My dad.* He was here. He was leaning against his green car, arms crossed over his chest, just outside in the parking area. I felt like fainting. Instead, I turned and began sprinting as fast as I could in the opposite direction. Blake came chasing after me and took me home.

This wasn't turning out at all as I had envisioned.

Outside the courtroom, Rosa tried to gather herself. It wasn't looking good. The hours were quickly passing, and it was growing more discouraging all the time. My parents' court-appointed attorney was pushing to convict me as a criminal runaway and send me back to Ohio, bypassing the Florida court altogether. And they seemed to be gaining traction. Rosa sighed, void of energy. So much was at stake.

The direct route to justice didn't seem to be working. But she still had one more ace to play, and she didn't have very much time in which to play it. Standing in the parking lot of the courthouse, she whispered a little prayer—*Please let this work, Lord!*—and clicked Send on her telephone.

Time would tell. In a hurry.

The summer breeze was heavy and humid as I sat on the deck of the Lorenzes' home, praying and pondering my future while getting ready for what would become birthday surprise number three.

Rosa had sent a press release to the local Orlando news stations. Her last-ditch strategy was to get media exposure for my story, circumventing DCF's efforts to keep everything quiet and cycle me out of the system with as little fuss as possible. If we could stoke public support, the court and some of the behind-the-scenes players would need to think twice before treating me as an average runaway kid rebelling against her parents.

Beverly came on the deck and handed me a phone. "Hey, little sista!" the caller said. *Brian!* Hearing his voice made me miss him even more. It brought back so many memories.

"Hey, B," I responded.

"I am so glad you're all right, Rifqa. You just tell them the truth, okay? Don't sugarcoat anything."

"I won't. But be praying."

"Of course I will."

And I could sense those prayers as the phalanx of cameramen, reporters, and photographers began assembling in the Lorenzes' living room. I had been alerted by Rosa that the press had been summoned, but I didn't expect it to be *this*. I walked into the hubbub, still sporting my new white dress, drowning in raw nerves at being the center of such rabid attention.

Migdalia, an investigator for DCF, had gotten wind of Rosa's stratagem and had arrived on the front porch, demanding to put a stop to it. She did not want me talking to the press without getting official permission from the state, and she was there to inform me that I *did not* have it! But with Beverly's mother and Rosa guarding the door, Migdalia was fighting a losing battle against two determined opponents. "What other cases are you working on?" Rosa asked, using small talk to distract her.

"She can't be interviewed, Rosa, unless she gets permission. Stop!" she yelled to the television people. "Stop!"

But you don't stop journalists who smell a good story and don't back off at the sight of government officials who look like they're trying to suppress the truth. Migdalia could only watch helplessly as a microphone was shoved in my face and I was given a platform to share my story, not only with Orlando, but ultimately with America.

And I did. Unashamedly.

I was scared out of my mind, but Blake stood beside me, placing a strong arm around me for support. I answered their questions as directly as possible, knowing I was fighting for my life and knowing it felt like a joke to the cameramen and reporters who were listening. They couldn't understand. But the people who'd be watching, maybe *they* would.

"What do you want, Rifqa?" That was the bottom-line question they asked.

"What do I want? I want to be free to worship Jesus. I want to be able to read my Bible and go to church on Sunday and say 'Jesus is alive' whenever I want to. I want to worship Jesus freely! *That's* what I want!"

Within a matter of hours, but ahead of my rescheduled hearing, my story hit the international wires. Viral. The media and commentary, as it continued to spin out, could be cruel at times, but the support far outweighed the doubters and detractors. Orlando was in an uproar. Few people were rooting for my parents, and many were rooting for my freedom. Rosa's plan worked. I now had a fighting chance. By drawing attention to my story, nothing could now be done secretively in the courtroom. Whatever decision the magistrate made would be printed in every newspaper in town and around the nation.

They'd better get it right.

Twenty-Three

August 10, 2009, 3:11 p.m.

Clerk: "In the interest of Bary, please state your appearances for the record."

"Krista Bartholomew, guardian ad litem program."

"Migdalia Santini, investigator for the department."

"Dave Husted, attorney with the state of Florida."

"Barbara Joyner, attorney for the father."

"Craig McCarthy, attorney for the mother."

Krista said, "It is my understanding that the child and the attorney of the child are here."

Judge Adams looked up from her stack of paperwork and asked, "Where are the child and the child's attorney?"

"Yes, Rosa Armesto, attorney for the child."

"Thank you, Ms. Armesto. Where is the child?"

Everything seemed a blur at first. The faces, the people, the clicking of cameras. I wanted to be invisible. Yet every eye in the place appeared to be fixed on me, including those of my father, who I expected to be there but whose actions I couldn't predict, and so I couldn't predict my reaction to him either.

Seeing him up close again for the first time since hearing what I believed to be threats to kill me, I wanted to scream. I shuddered at the sight of him, which unnerved me even more. Could the people in this room who looked so official yet knew so little about who I was, what I'd faced, and what I would be facing next if they chose to herd me through without hearing me out, could they really force me to return to my mother and father? Back to a nightmare I'd never wake up from?

"Is this Fatima?" the judge asked.

I nodded, taking my seat, responding to the formality of being called by my first name.

Florida's attorney Dave Husted was the first to speak and lay the groundwork for the proceedings. His hair was salt and pepper, mostly salt. His demeanor struck me as disinterested and impatient. Coldly abrupt. Just wanting to get this over with.

"We have been in contact with the state of Ohio, and they have an open investigation as we do. We propose that the child be transported into the custody of the department in Ohio. They have agreed to take the child and do an investigation to find out whether it's safe for the child to be returned to her parents or not."

Again, this was the state's wash-our-hands position: to present me as a simple runaway, a flash of headstrong teenage angst and misunderstanding. They just wanted to send me back to where I came from, to get me out of Florida and out of their hair. He didn't seem to care about my side of the story.

But his wasn't the only voice. The judge went from counsel to counsel, listening to each position and appeal. Rosa, of course, urged the court to take emergency jurisdiction, to recognize that sending me home put me in grave danger.

"What's the dad's position?" the judge asked.

"The father can arrange transportation back to Ohio," his attorney answered, "not in his custody, but for the child to be delivered to the children's agency in Ohio. I spoke to two people at the attorney general's clearinghouse there who work with the missing children's department. They were under the impression that arrangements have already been made for the child to be taken back to Ohio."

"Mr. McCarthy? Mom's position?"

"She supports what counsel for the father has stated. Asking the court to dismiss both shelter and dependency petition. Does not think either of those petitions are sufficient. Ideally, mother would like to take her child back. If the court is inclined to grant emergency jurisdiction to the state, mother would like the child to be placed back in the home state of Ohio."

I'm not saying I'm proud of this, but I honestly wanted to throw something at both of my parents' attorneys. And at Mr. Husted too. Their three-way push to send me home, while certainly within their rights to propose, riled me at the rank injustice of it. Their voices were stoic and cold. So unsympathetic toward my valid reasons for running away from home in fear of my life. I was screaming on the inside, *Someone save me!* Yet they had no idea they were acting as advocates of injustice and oppression by what they were saying. I wished with every ounce of my being they could see the truth. But it didn't matter, because from what I gathered, they simply did not care.

The judge addressed Rosa again: "What's your position of the child going from our DCF to Ohio DCF?"

"I would be opposed to it because it would not be in the best interest of the child. There is a very strong, active Muslim community in Ohio, and she is in fear for her life that if taken back to Ohio, and eventually returned to her parents, they will send her back to her country of origin where she will definitely be killed for being a Christian."

The judge listened to all sides. "GAL's position?" she asked, looking at Ms. Bartholomew.

The role of the guardian ad litem is to recommend what he or she deems the best interest of a minor child, according to the law, but not necessarily to speak for what the child wants as a client in the way a representing attorney like Rosa would. So while I wasn't sure whether to trust this confident lady with piercing blue eyes, she seemed to be on my side, and her presence made me feel safer, especially when she answered.

"Your Honor, at this point there are really two issues before the court.

The first one is emergency jurisdiction. I think no matter how you look at it, you do have a child here who is absolutely terrified, which does give you probable cause for emergency jurisdiction. So I believe the most appropriate placement at this time is a form of mutual placement, which would be department care. I would advocate foster care. If Ohio is not interested, this court absolutely has the power to keep jurisdiction here."

"I have contacted the Ohio court," the judge responded, "but have been unsuccessful in speaking with the judge."

"Then I suggest we set a hearing three weeks out to see if Ohio is interested in taking the case. If the Ohio court does not want to exercise jurisdiction, it is up to the Florida court."

Everyone had now presented their concise opinions and requests. Everything now rested in the experienced, analytical mind of the judge, who paused for a brief moment in what had already been a long day.

After a long pause, she said, with sweeping finality, "The court is going to exercise emergency jurisdiction over the child. *I* will shelter the child. The child is in the care of the Department of Children and Families."

I sighed in exhaustion. I would stay in Florida, away from my parents—at least for now.

Twenty-Four

Within a matter of hours I was rolling a suitcase containing all my possessions into a large, institutional, barracks-style room with lots of beds lined up along both walls. One room was for girls; one room was for boys; neither room did it for me. I hated it already.

Group homes are the modern equivalent of the old-style *Oliver Twist* orphanage: a place for underage kids who have no place to call home, only worse because nearly all the kids living there would be in foster care if they hadn't been kicked out of their families for their unbearable behavior. Imagine herding them all into one place and being made to share space with them. It's sure not summer youth camp.

But this was my temporary new home after being forced to choose the lesser of two evils: life in a Florida group home rather than life at home with my family in Ohio. I was prohibited from living with or even seeing the Lorenzes, who were now under investigation for housing a minor without permission of her parents. The judge's order placed me in custody of the state's foster system, which started in this cattle-barn of a bedroom until a place opened up for me in a foster family's home.

Thankfully, no one else was there when I first walked in, so I was able to vent my full first impression without tempering it for an audience. I threw my stuff on the floor and wept, quietly yelling at God for the indignity of this arrangement. I didn't want to cause a scene, didn't want to alert the people in charge to a disturbance in the house, but I was seething in anger, having briefly tasted the joys of a real family only to see it all stripped away. What a cruel joke! I had never felt more alone, not even when locked away by myself in the juvenile jail cell. I felt so abandoned, so betrayed.

After falling onto my bed of depression, I stared up at the ceiling. A

Bible verse entered my mind. I recited it, first with a hint of mockery and then as a plea, "Though He slay me, yet will I trust in Him," aching to believe these words of Job. But death in that moment seemed better than the reality I was living in. And as anger rolled up and over me, I thrashed with rage on the bed, punching and pounding, kicking and throwing the comforter and pillow I was lying on. I hated this. I couldn't believe it. I had no idea how long I'd be stuck here with nowhere else to lay my head but this miserable bed of tears.

Things began to look up almost immediately, however. My caseworker, Migdalia, took me to the DCF building the next day and told me they'd found a foster family for me. My first reaction was to think how much I missed Blake and Beverly. But a young spiffy woman soon arrived, pushing a stroller and hauling baby gear through the slender doorway where I was waiting. A little girl toddled behind her. "Come on, honey," she said to her daughter, "we don't got all day," in a pleasant but thick southern accent. I stared at her and tried to appraise her. She looked to be in her late thirties. Pretty green eyes radiated warmth beneath her short, straight brown hair. She came across the room and pulled me into a warm, kind embrace—not at all what I was expecting.

I guess she's my new foster mom?

And she was great. The way I had it figured, as I settled into their amazing home, I'd be staying with this sweet family for as long as I was in Florida.

But that's not the way foster care was going to work for me. Due to the international attention and local publicity garnered by my unusual case and story, my living arrangements were supposed to be kept secret—a state of anonymity that rarely held for long before word somehow leaked out. So DCF continually moved me from foster home to foster home, primarily and presumably for security reasons. At other times some of the families would back out on their own, not wanting to risk their lives or those of the other kids under their care by housing a girl who believed her life was in danger.

Some of the foster homes were nightmarish. Others were tolerable, though none were ideal. They weren't really homes to me, just random buildings to sleep, eat, and bathe in. After a while I kept my stuff always packed and ready to move, basically living out of a suitcase.

And through all the upheaval and turmoil of my living conditions, the legal hearings and shenanigans that were becoming my crazy life continued to spin confusedly through the judicial system. The frantic speed of strategizing and information gathering was matched only by the laborious drag of the process. Moves and countermoves were constantly waged, considered, reviewed, and implemented behind the scenes by busy people on both sides of the issue, all of which were being intensified by political overtones that soon glommed on to the proceedings and complicated them even more.

For a situation that had gotten out of hand enough to force my initial running away from home, I could never have imagined just how far out of hand it would ultimately go.

One evening while sitting on the bed in whatever foster home I was occupying at the time, I was tapping around on my laptop and soon thinking back to the night when my father came so close to hitting me with it. The thought made me wonder what people were saying about my family and my case. Up until this time—ever since that day at the Lorenzes when I'd been shocked by what a simple Internet search had revealed about my notoriety—I'd avoided reading anything that had been written about me. But giving in to curiosity, I Googled my name just to see. Thousands of clickable options appeared. Unbelievable.

Scanning through only the brief summaries that appeared on the Google pages, I was stunned at the reporting and interpretations of my case. Choosing one, an article from the Assyrian International News

Agency titled "Honor Killings Come to America," I allowed myself to press deeper and read the full account, which included this quote:

> David Miller Smith of *Pakistan Daily* . . . wrote an article about
> the dispute on August 15, titled "Pregnant Minor Lanka Girl
> Kidnapped by Ohio Christian Church—Brainwashed Against
> Parents Forcibly Converted." The report claims that Fathima's
> parents said she was using drugs and engaging in sexual communi-
> cation with middle-aged men online. "When the parents tried to
> control her behavior she refused to do so. On her return to the
> home she conjured up a story of conversion to Christianity. . . .
> How many more girls will the church kidnap?"

What?

Kidnapped? No, I'd been desperate to run away and leave home. *Drugs?* I've never touched them, ever. *Pregnant? Promiscuous behavior?* My friends at school could attest I'd never even had a boyfriend, much less done anything promiscuous.

So is this how it works when you're public fodder? People can make up anything they want and then print it as fact? I was just a teenage girl want-ing to live for Jesus. That's it! None of this stuff was anywhere close to being true. I was furious at the inaccuracies and worried at the effect it might have on my future.

How do you fight back in a war like this . . . and win?

Twenty-Five

Neither person was happy either to hear it or to say it, but Rosa didn't have any choice. She was sitting with Blake and Beverly, and her body language mirrored her anxiety before she'd even put the bad news into words: "I'm sorry, but I can't proceed with Rifqa's case."

"What?!" cried Blake and Beverly simultaneously. "We have no one else who'll take it, Rosa. Why are you backing down now?"

"It's very complicated, but to put it in simple terms, one of the attorneys that was appointed to represent her parents works for the same agency that I do. And it's against the law for two attorneys, each affiliated with the same firm, to contend against each other in a proceeding. It's considered a conflict of interest. I could lose my job by going forward with this. However, I do know someone who might be able to help us: a fine and experienced attorney named John Stemberger."

"No." Blake's demeanor sank even further. "I and several local officials have spoken with John already, actually. He is well known and has litigated several high-profile civil cases, but he said he's not an expert in dependency law."

"I know," Rosa interjected, "but *I've* spoken with him as well. And he has volunteered as a guardian ad litem representing abused and neglected children for thirteen years, so I convinced him that I would help with the research and writing on the substantive legal issues behind the scenes, and he would litigate the case, representing you in court."

This still didn't sound quite right to Blake and Beverly, but if there were no other alternative . . .

"Okay then," Blake said. "You think it'll work?"

"It'll work."

"And you'll tell Rifqa? She's going to be disappointed."

I really was. I'd grown so attached to Rosa. She was one of the only advocates on my side. But I trusted her judgment on what she thought was best, and I knew she was only doing what she needed to do. When she called to tell me about it, she told me John was willing to take my case pro bono and represent me in the courtroom. "But it's totally up to you, sweetie, whatever you want to do. I hope you'll at least talk to him, though, before you make your decision."

If I'd known what an amazing friend and counselor John would become to me over the next several months and years, I wouldn't have needed even a phone call before saying yes. But if *he'd* known what was coming, he might have wished he'd stayed as far away from my case as possible.

Nearly two weeks passed before my next hearing, which meant the unsettledness of my situation continued to loom over me with no way to alleviate the dread. Anything could still happen. The chance of my being sent back to my parents remained all too real.

The path of least resistance remained the most likely prediction of how the judge might rule, forcing me back to Ohio. But Rosa's brazenly bold maneuver to incite a public outcry over my situation had turned me into a hot-button issue with the governors and senators whose jobs depended on being sure the public approves of what they're doing.

This was about to get wild.

I was coming in from a doctor's appointment on Friday, August 21, knowing it was nearly time for me to get ready for my second court hearing. But the scene in my foster family's home wasn't the typical bustle of cute kids running around. The mood in the house was artificially proper and in order, as if ruled by some unspoken secret I hadn't yet been told. Two older men in shiny dark suits greeted me as I entered. *Who are these people, and why are they here?* I wondered.

"Hello, Rifqa," said the first. "It's a pleasure to finally meet you in person. We're from the Florida Department of Children and Families." Then gesturing toward a huge, bald, muscularly built man in sunglasses, he said, "Pablo here is a well-trained bodyguard and will be escorting you to the courthouse today. The press will be packing the courtroom, and we want to make sure you're safely out of harm's way."

It was like a movie. Pablo barely spoke, doing all his talking with the intimidating aura of his presence, standing there waiting for orders with his hands neatly clasped together.

Okay then. (I guess.)

I went into my foster sister's room to get ready. I couldn't decide what to wear. After cycling in and out of several outfit choices with her help, I decided to stick with a navy suit, and walked out to where my entourage was dutifully waiting.

"I'm ready!" I announced, proudly strutting in with straightened dark hair and my Bible under one arm. Silent, stoic Pablo simply nodded and pointed to the door, which he opened to reveal a dark, undercover police car parked and running in the driveway. As we approached it, he stepped in front of me and held the car door while I climbed into the backseat. *I can't believe I have a bodyguard!*

As we drove away, he turned to me from the front seat and said in a deep, authoritative voice, "Don't worry. I'm going to keep you safe." I believed him. But something still seemed odd about the whole thing. Why all this sudden concern for my safety from some governmental agency? It felt like someone using a sledgehammer to kill an ant—far too much firepower for the job.

Soon, though, as we arrived at the rear of the courthouse, my focus shifted from the heavy-duty security of my transportation detail to the unknowns of what was coming up. Garage-like doors opened and closed as we entered an enclosed parking lot surrounded by barbed wire. A small cluster of men escorted me inside, where for hours we waited in the judge's chambers for the hearing to begin, along with my new attorney, John, and my guardian ad litem, Krista.

I was getting so nervous! Krista tried to lighten the mood by making jokes. And I tried distracting myself by teasing Pablo until I finally extracted a small smile from him, asking question after question to get him to talk. But the scene grew even more disquieting when another group of men walked in, again looking highly important and impressed with themselves.

What's up with these guys and their shiny suits?

Something just felt fishy. They shook my hand and gave me hugs as though they were my grandpa or long-lost uncle. "Rifqa! It's a pleasure to meet you," said the main one. "My name is George Sheldon. I'm the secretary of the Department of Children and Families, and I've been appointed by Florida governor Charlie Crist to your case. The governor wanted to be here today but couldn't. He extends his apologies. But we all want to make sure Florida takes care of you well. We are committed to your safety, and we stand behind you 100 percent. Hey, by the way, have you ever been to Disney World?"

Ohhh-kay. It was kind of funny, really. Just a couple of weeks ago, locked up in jail for doing nothing wrong except trying to protect myself, I was mocked and ridiculed by the low-paid, run-of-the-mill guards who brought me to my first hearing. And now I was garnering the attention of the governor and receiving personal, wall-to-wall protection while the highest authorities in the state were assuring me of their commitment to fight by my side.

Even Marco Rubio, who at the time was running against Governor Charlie Crist for the United States Senate seat in Florida, made a statement in support of my safety. He said, "It is imperative that state officials use every legal tool at their disposal to properly evaluate Rifqa's best interests. Florida has a responsibility not only to protect her innocent life but also to defend her sacred right to worship freely."

Wow!

Still, I couldn't help but feel there was more going on than met the eye.

Finally my time to appear in court had arrived. As we wound through corridors on the way to the courtroom, Pablo said to me, "Listen, if anything happens, I throw you on my back and I run. Just don't fight me, okay? My job is to keep you safe."

I nodded and moved forward. I was terrified. I took a few deep breaths and clutched my Bible tighter. It gave me a sense of safety as I walked into the room.

But if I thought I'd been the center of attention the last time I'd stood in this place, I was totally unprepared for how much more feverish the media storm had grown. You'd have thought I was on *Entertainment Tonight* or something. The only sound I could hear upon entering the room were large cameras ferociously clicking away, followed each time by strobes of flashing bright lights. It was blinding, disturbing. Every move, every word, even the way I was dressed was being logged in reporters' notebooks as I scooted toward my assigned chair. I felt so incredibly awkward and out of reality. I had no preset for knowing how to process all the attention.

When order was called, the commotion in the gallery stilled to an anxious quiet, broken only by scattered, muted clearings of an occasional throat. The proceeding opened with volleys of legal terms and preludes I didn't understand. But before we could even get to what I thought to be the purpose of the hearing—determining which state would claim jurisdiction over my custody—a DCF attorney said, "Judge, we have a petition for a motion to disqualify the minor's counsel."

John, seated next to me, abruptly peeled off his reading glasses in utter disbelief and gasped, "What?!" In a case of one-after-another unexpected developments, this was perhaps the most unexpected of all: the unusual tactic of one party trying to disqualify the other party's attorney. I'm told the relationship between a lawyer and his client is one of the most legally sacred things that is above being challenged by anyone other than the client. But now they were coming after my new lawyer? It didn't make any sense at all.

It was another bizarre turn in what had become a high-profile and very controversial legal proceeding.

Judge Dawson looked with puzzlement toward the DCF attorney, waiting for an explanation.

"Judge, we believe the minor child already has a lawyer through the guardian ad litem. Not to mention, Mr. Stemberger is associated with a national advocacy group, and we believe it would be in the best interest of the child to keep religion out of this."

Enraged, John bolted upright from his seat. "I object, Your Honor! This is ridiculous! My client has the right to choose whomever she wants to appoint as her counsel. Even minor girls who are trying to get an abortion without parental consent have the right to a lawyer!"

What could possibly be behind this? I couldn't figure it out. All I knew, sitting there, was that the state was trying to silence the only voice left who was arguing for my position and who believed my life was genuinely at risk because of the religious views of my parents and their mosque. And how did this square with the events of the day: the DCF secretary, the bodyguard, the governor, the whole nine yards of official assurances? If John were pushed out of the picture, DCF would own the courtroom, and I'd be left to fight with one arm tied behind my back. Could it be that George Sheldon and Governor Crist were the ones playing this legal card, wanting to put forward a public face of defending the poor Muslim girl who's not allowed to practice her Christianity while simultaneously working the back channels to get this whole publicity mess back to Ohio? I didn't know. I still don't. But it sure made me wonder.

John, for his part, was proving to me that Rosa was exactly right about him. He was bold and articulate, and I knew in that moment that he would not shy away from defending me and aggressively fighting for my safety. I felt he really understood me, cared about me, and believed in my story. And though I could barely hide my fear, his dogged presence at my side gave me confidence.

Judge Dawson took a minute to look at the petition while the room heated with whispers and side conversation. "I rule that the minor child still has a right to counsel," he said, tapping his gavel against the sound block, causing it to resonate throughout the room. With a sigh of relief, John responded, "Thank you, Judge."

"Okay," Judge Dawson said, looking at the next stack of papers in his hands. "Next filed motion?"

These judicial hearings can become so complicated and never-ending. This next motion had something to do with the Florida Department of Law Enforcement agreeing to do a preliminary investigation into my account of what had happened, but needing two weeks before being able to come back with any findings on any credible threats to my life and person.

John, of course, stayed alert and in the mix, responding to every new swing of activity in the courtroom by trying to bring the focus back to where it belonged and ensure I wasn't going to be thrown back into danger.

As for me, my head was swimming with all the legal language, and I tried to disconnect from it by reading my Bible. I had it open in my lap: "The voice of the LORD is over the waters; the God of glory thunders; the LORD is over many waters. The voice of the LORD is powerful; the voice of the LORD is full of majesty. The voice of the LORD breaks the cedars. . . . The voice of the LORD divides the flames of fire. . . . The LORD sat enthroned at the Flood, and the LORD sits as King forever. The LORD will give strength to His people; the LORD will bless His people with peace" (Psalm 29:3–5, 7, 10–11).

These hearings and their implications terrified me. My life was hanging in the balance of a judicial system that demanded I prove the validity of my abuse while seeming to begin from a position that seriously doubted I was telling the truth. I closed my eyes, needing peace, letting these declarations of God's power flood over me, and just started to pray.

Jesus, I can't do this alone. Thank You that it's You who holds all of creation. It's You who made the stars. It's You who put breath in my lungs. You are my King and Judge. Help me trust You, Lord. You are the one who makes the final call.

A serene sense of His presence filled me in the midst of all the chaos and stress, even as I could begin to hear a slow dribble of rain begin to dance on the roof above the courtroom. Soon the sprinkles reached a rather thunderous roar that made each participant in the hearing need to talk a little louder to be heard over it. My eyes fell again on those words of Scripture—"The voice of the LORD is over the waters; the God of glory thunders"—and I melted as best as I could into His eternally strong embrace.

Then the subject turned to what was proving to be the real sticking point: immigration. "I'm confused," the judge said. "Is she a US citizen or not?"

Krista answered, "I have put in a significant amount of time to evaluate the child's immigration status. I have asked parents' counsel numerous times to provide information, but information has not been given. They have not yielded any proof that she is legally in the US."

The judge looked beyond Krista and spoke directly to my father, who was seated among the audience. "Dad, how is she here?"

"She came here in 2000 on a B1B2 visa and changed to L1L2," he said, "and right now she is out of status. She needs to get adjusted."

"Does she have documentation? Does she have a passport?"

"Yes, we can provide it to the court."

Round and round it went. And so another frustrating flurry of motions and assignments and requests for new information ended with no firm conclusions, with no more closure on my status and future than when I'd showed up that afternoon under Pablo's watchful eye. Court was dismissed and the waiting game continued.

But the political game commenced immediately.

Shortly thereafter Governor Crist issued a press release:

I am grateful to Circuit Judge Daniel Dawson for his decision
to grant Fathima [*sic*] Rifqa Bary the right to remain in Florida.
The first and only priority of my administration is the safety and
wellbeing of this child. I am grateful for the good work of Department of Children and Families Secretary George Sheldon . . . for
personally advocating the administration's position by attending
today's hearing. We will continue to fight to protect Rifqa's safety
and wellbeing as we move forward.

My first-blush impression, upon reading this, was to feel extremely
comforted. Wow, I had adults with such incredible power rooting for me.
But I began to suspect in the coming days that while Governor Crist and
his administration were trying to spin my story into a political victory for
his campaign, my own victory in this case wasn't really of much concern
to them. Every time Fox News reported on my story, they were asking
listeners nationwide to call Governor Crist's office and tell him to fight to
keep me in Florida and not allow me to be sent back to my parents in
Ohio. The governor was doing a good job of trying to publicly appease the
thousands around the nation who were calling and e-mailing and pressur-
ing him to keep me in Orlando. But the reality in the courtroom was the
state agency that reported directly to him, DCF, was doing things directly
to the contrary, trying to get the pressure off him (and his campaign) by
sending me back to Ohio.

And the more I learned about how this was going down, the madder
it made me.

A few days later, what seemed like a small army of Florida law enforcement
officials arrived at my foster home, removing me to a secure location where

they grilled me and recorded me for more than two hours about my life, my memories, and my complaints against my family and what they had threatened to do to me for practicing my Christian faith. Visibly armed with semiautomatic weapons, and with only one female in the group, the investigation team badgered and taunted me with tough-nosed questions. It all came down to one question: "You don't really think your dad would've killed you, do you?" It had all the earmarks of someone trying to break down a witness.

And they were doing a pretty good job of it too. At one point, in tears, I asked them, "What's going to happen to me?" It just seemed like they were trying to paint a picture as if I were no more than a troubled, rebellious teenager.

"Oh, we don't know!" they heartlessly laughed, further ganging up with the strong-arm intimidation.

The most stunning part of this interrogation was that it was done without the presence, knowledge, or even notification of my lawyer or even my guardian ad litem. John Stemberger was in Miami at the time, but when he found out about this "interview" after the fact, he was furious. They clearly were taking advantage of me and trying to lead me to some specific conclusions. Furthermore, the officers were from the Florida Department of Law Enforcement (FDLE). And guess which executive official in Florida directly oversees the FDLE? Governor Charlie Crist.

All of this investigation into my case was happening here—in Florida. None of it was happening where the problem was—in Ohio. So I grew more apprehensive than ever as the following weeks unfolded, dotted every two weeks or so with another hearing, another round of musical chairs, with rules seemingly made up on the fly to make it as complicated as it could possibly be.

It was extremely rare, I was told, to have two courts in two different states, with two judges presiding and calling to order two separate hearings connected via speaker phone over the same legal issue. The legal question they were trying to resolve is whether Florida or Ohio had jurisdiction in my case to resolve the dependency question that determined if I would be returned to my parents or declared a dependent in need of the state's protection. The legal fight was also for custody over a minor who didn't have legal status in America, which I didn't, since my parents had never sought citizenship or applied for extensions to their temporary visas. This made the legal hearing even more unique, catching the attention of both the national and international media.

My immigration status again dominated the first of these final two hearings, with Krista holding up a piece of paper that was assumed to be my mother's passport. But the photocopy was so poor that its authenticity couldn't be verified. And even if it could, the document appeared to have expired four years prior. Other information the court had ordered my parents to supply had not been forthcoming at all, so the judge had no recourse other than to schedule another hearing and demand that these documents be presented within ten working days. My parents' and their lawyers' unwillingness to cooperate was only making things more complicated and difficult.

But there was method to their madness because, bottom line, if we had been able to wrap up the loose ends of my case in a timely fashion— even with its unprecedented challenges—I thought we appeared to be on the verge of prevailing. The judge had seemed to be more or less proving sympathetic toward my plight. We'd been able to somewhat clear away the noise and distractions and zero in on the main goal: getting a Florida court to issue a decision that gave Florida legal custody over me until I turned eighteen. It was as hard as that and as simple as that.

And yet my parents, buying time with delay tactics, found a way to turn the tables on justice and logic. After the third or fourth legal filing, they filed a quasi-criminal charge through their newly selected attorneys to accuse me of being an "unruly minor." Although I had technically done nothing illegal, running away from home could be considered a criminal misdemeanor in Ohio. And once the state of Ohio officially entered the picture, this meant a new court proceeding could send me back.

Well, great.

Now the case could legally be transferred to Ohio, which is what a lot of people obviously wanted to happen anyway. And so when we arrived at the final hearing in Florida—Monday, September 21, 2009—I ended up crying in the arms of my caseworkers the majority of the time. I was sick and tired of the pressure and frightened and angry that I had again been bullied against my will through my father's manipulative measures. I sat there unashamedly allowing the tears to roll down my cheeks while the women on my team stroked my hair and rubbed my shoulders.

My parents had found a loophole, and it meant I was headed back to Ohio. I'd still be under the state's custody as a minor, but I'd be that much closer to being ensnared by whatever legal web of lies might get me back into that apartment under my father and the mosque's reign of terror.

And they wouldn't stop weaving until they had achieved that bitter end.

Twenty-Six

They came for me in the night. The *middle* of the night. My foster mother had told me (without telling me why) that I wasn't allowed to know when or how my transfer to Ohio would take place. The high-profile nature of my situation, coupled with the court's fear that I might possibly run away to avoid being relocated closer to home, meant that the travel arrangements were kept secret even from me. I was instructed to keep my bags packed and ready to go.

So I shouldn't have been surprised when she woke me up at three in the morning on a Tuesday, alerting me that men were here to take me. "Hurry up, sweetie. Get ready."

They certainly didn't seem to mind who knew about it *that* night. Police officers surrounded my foster home while the sheriff whisked me into what seemed to be a military vehicle of some sort, and we sped off into the darkness with cruisers escorting us front and rear. The state officials may have downplayed the potential danger I was in publicly in the court-room, but privately they were taking it very seriously. I was soon en route to Ohio on a commercial airliner, accompanied by a brusque, business-like sheriff and my caseworker, Maxine, whose comforting presence somewhat offset the sheriff's uncomfortable company.

We had been in the air for a couple of hours or more when we began our descent. This had certainly been a much quicker trip than my two-day bus ride, the last time I covered this same ground in reverse. As the plane lowered in altitude and prepared to land, I noticed through the window that we weren't even at an airport. We'd touched down in a wide-open area with several white buildings framing a lone landing strip. Confused whispers began trickling through the aisle as other passengers, noticing the unexpected detour, began to fear that something was wrong.

"Sorry, folks," the captain's voice pinged through the intercom, "we've had a slight delay. There's nothing wrong with the plane. We just need to take care of a small, brief matter, and we'll be right back on our way. Won't take but a moment."

The sheriff motioned for me to get up. Maxine wrapped an arm around me and guided me down the aisle, the officer pressing close behind. A flight attendant opened the door, but instead of walking into the inside of an airport, I was hustled down a flight of stairs to the ground below, while the deafening whir of helicopter blades pulsated overhead. I covered my ears while my long hair whipped and flapped across my face, and a pretty television reporter and cameraman approached, film rolling. She turned to face the camera, with me and my entourage positioned behind her in the background, and announced for the local news viewers, "We've got her," as the sheriff hustled me into a waiting police car.

Could this get much weirder? Or much worse?

But it could. In the car was a woman named Carol, who introduced herself to me as my new caseworker. She was an older lady with short, fading blond hair and a quiet detachment in her demeanor. Her first words to me, after the customary greetings and sharing of information, were, "Well, Rifqa, are you ready to see your parents?"

Her words cut me like a knife. I'm sure I visibly bristled. I didn't know if she was trying to be mean or sickeningly sarcastic. If she was referring to my *real* parents, she obviously hadn't gotten the memo about why I was in this undesirable position to begin with, or else she didn't believe I needed protection from them. If she was referring to my new foster parents, what made her think I was looking forward to meeting people who would probably care less about me than *she* did? I didn't see anything to be excited about.

But that's what I could come to expect from Carol. If she'd been a

more compassionate person, knowing the condition of the home where I
was about to be placed, she wouldn't have asked if I was ready to see my
parents. She would've given me something more along the lines of a warning and a tetanus shot.

We were nowhere near New Albany, either by geography or demographic, as we drove through a dark, gloomy neighborhood before rolling
to a stop at a run-down house. Martha, an emotionless woman with curly
hair and a stern countenance, greeted me at the door and pointed up the
stairway. "Your room's to the left," she said, revealing a few missing teeth.
Sizing up the environment as I inched inside with my small collection of
belongings, I saw a large bald man seated nearby on a sofa. He barely
turned to acknowledge my existence before clearing his throat and refo-
cusing on his television program.

It's just temporary, Rifqa, I told myself. *You won't be here forever.
They'll be moving you around from place to place, just like they did in
Florida. Be tough, girl. It'll be all right.*

But trying not to despair or want to run away was hard. The room
given to me was eerie and cold. It seemed hardly any larger than a walk-in
closet. The bed linens reeked of sourness and body odor, and the walls
were pummeled with holes the size of softballs, or perhaps (it seemed)
about the circumference of an angry fist.

Suddenly a timid, pale voice surprised me from the lower berth of the
bunk bed.

"Hi."

Oh, great. I've got company. I can't even suffer in solitude.

"My name's Amelia," she said, her face looking older than her voice
sounded.

But maybe it was good that I wasn't alone. Otherwise I might've immediately thrown my bag on the floor, thrown myself across the bed, and
thrown the same kind of fit I'd let loose at the group home where I'd first
been assigned in Florida. Having a roommate stood my emotions back to

their feet. It steadied me with the reminder that God was in this place too, and that I was here to live out the change He'd crafted in my heart, a power and love I'd considered worth risking my life for. His truth could reign in this tiny, creepy room with Amelia just as He had reigned in the many places and over the many details that had led me here and would keep me safe. I was sure of it.

I slowly and methodically unpacked and put away my clothes. I unrolled each dress while humming to myself the lyrics of one of my favorite worship songs, both asking and promising the Lord to help me be a living sanctuary, even in this living hell.

My time there wasn't as temporary as I'd hoped, however. I ended up staying for a number of months, and Martha's rules of the house made it seem even longer than that. I couldn't leave my bedroom after ten o'clock at night, even to walk to the kitchen for a drink of water. I couldn't talk on the phone or visit with anyone who wasn't thoroughly cleared through background checks and included on an approved list of contacts. Using the wrong pot on the stove or leaving something of mine in the living room could invoke a blistering, angry lecture. Even though her husband looked physically intimidating, he wasn't as verbally and emotionally abusive as *she* could be. It wasn't as bad as my life at home had been, but it did have its similarities.

My only relief (if you could call it that) was the escape of the school day, except that the makeup of the charter school I was forced to attend could hardly have been more different than New Albany High. Sixty percent of the student population had done jail time, which, I guess, included me as well. And yet a large number of the girls were either pregnant or already single moms. Even with my own unorthodox, unsavory story, I was seen as the rich kid in the pink cardigan and skinny jeans, the out-of-place preppy in a hallway full of juvenile delinquents.

Just to give you a taste: my first day on campus included a mandatory lockdown (one of the students had brought a firearm to school), as well as an emergency, school-wide assembly where the principal slammed the door behind himself and yelled, "When are you kids going to get your act together?!"

The coursework in this school was ridiculously easy. I ended up earning nearly double the number of credits that most of the others would complete. By the time I finished, I'd covered two years of material in a little more than six months. But at least the diversion of study gave me something else to think about besides my living conditions, and each day drew me nearer to the magic moment when I would turn eighteen and be legally free from this manipulative control. Each night, however, I would lie under the covers in my cold bedroom, hating the dehumanizing trauma of my life, crying from the pain that never totally lifted from my heart.

One particularly lonely, empty night, I reached toward the frost-covered window that chilled the room with its drafty, unsealed edges and drew a small cross in the wintery fog on the glass. Underneath, I noticed where another child had engraved "Get me out of here" on the windowsill.

I apparently hadn't been the first to feel this way.

The all-too-frequent revulsion of foster care never grew any easier to stomach. This latest house of horrors was just another in a long list that stretched back to my experiences in Florida, where perhaps the worst of all had been my stay in a home where the father hid a dangerous secret from the outside world: unexpected, explosive rage.

Thud! Thud! Thud! We might hear him outside our window, smashing flower pots on the concrete patio in the backyard. *Bam! Bam! Bam!* Banging the back door. Coming in. Going out.

Relax, Rifqa, he's not going to do anything to hurt you. He's downstairs. You're safe. I looked over at Nina, my nine-year-old foster sister, fear in her eyes. "What's he doing? He's crazy!" she said. I hated the manipulation and power his anger held over us.

And this is where the government had placed me for my "security."

Why was this happening to me? Why could I not get away from these people? Why had my only chance at escaping the tyranny and death threats of my father led me to places that were only marginally more tolerable than my own home had been? Why couldn't I have just stayed at Blake and Beverly's where I was loved and protected and cared for as a daughter should be? I didn't know if I could make it to eighteen without losing my mind.

Then—God's gift to me at just the right time—along came Mara and Steve.

In one of the most pleasant surprises of my life, the state department in charge of my custody moved me to the home of a gentle, sweet, older couple whose own kids were already grown but who continued to care for foster children because it was their passion and expertise. Their home was unlike any other I'd ever lived in, a dream home for a foster child. Mara (or Mamaw, as we called her) had short, curly hair and simply oozed love with every look and expression. Steve (Papaw) wore dark glasses and a mischievous smile and had a knack for fun that sometimes delighted, sometimes exasperated his wife and yet always brought a playful warmth to their home and their relationship.

The rest of our little band of vagabonds included thirteen-year-old Isabella and eight-year-old Raven. With ocean-blue eyes and short, cropped brown hair, Raven was full of innocence and life. It wasn't uncommon to see me giving little Ravy piggyback rides as we soared through the house imagining ourselves as sailors. Or to sometimes cuddle with her in her bed when I would tuck her in at night. Or to catch Isabella taking funny pictures on my laptop when I wasn't looking. I would playfully pretend to be enraged, screaming "I'm gonna get you!" and then chase her around the house, only to end up crying in fits of hysterical laughter, collapsed on top of each other, exhausted from the chase.

We came from entirely different backgrounds, but we meshed about as seamlessly as any three outcasts could gel, with only a few small spats and disagreements to keep things spicy and interesting. This was evident one morning when Isabella walked in the door with Mamaw from a hair appointment. I shouldn't say Isabella casually walked in; she made sure to fluff her blond hair in my direction and do the catwalk thing. I looked at her and did a double take.

She had the exact same haircut as mine.

Overcome with annoyance, I crossed my arms and threw a mini-fit. "Mamaw! *Why* did Isabella have to get the same haircut as me?"

Mamaw's lips tugged into a smile. "It's her way of saying 'I want to be like big sissy Rifqa.' It's a compliment, Rifqa!"

She held her gaze on me, waiting to see if her point had gotten through. I rolled my eyes and walked away dramatically, throwing my hands in the air while Isabella yelled teasingly, "I wuv you, Riffy."

We were an outcast family but nonetheless a family.

Both of the other girls were feisty and adventurous in their own ways, and together we enjoyed a life that was almost normal. At least, it was the longest stretch of normal I'd ever experienced. We loved each other tremendously, and Mamaw and Papaw made sure nothing ever stood in the way of our togetherness for very long.

One evening, picking at my dinner, though not feeling particularly hungry, I asked Mamaw if I could be excused. "I know I've hardly eaten at all today," I said, "but my stomach just feels heavy and full. I think I'll go lie down for a while."

Feeling full turned into feeling really uncomfortable. Then feeling uncomfortable turned into feeling weak and dizzy, with stabs of pain knifing into my side. I fought my way to the bathroom, sure I was going to be sick.

That's when I noticed the blood.

Lots and lots of blood.

"Maaaaamaaaaaw!"

As quickly as they could throw me into the car and race to the hospital, I was surrounded by ER nurses and medical personnel, some of whom didn't try hiding the shock and urgency of what they were seeing. "What is it?!" I screamed, hysterical. "It hurts!"

"Sweetie, we need you to open your legs," said the head nurse as she gently pushed them apart.

I screamed as loud as I could. "No!" And tried to fight off the nurses. "I can't let you look! Don't touch me! Don't touch me! Stop!" My faith seemed a million miles away in that moment.

"This looks bad. We need to give her some morphine right away," said one nurse, whipping her face away from me to get the attention of the other nurse in the room.

"We're going to take care of you, sweetie," said the other nurse, trying to calm me down.

Tears slanted out of my eyes, running down the side of my face while I gasped and howled in agony. Soon after, as many as six doctors and a handful more nurses hustled into the room. One of them rubbed my arm while saying, "Relax, sweetie, this stuff is going to make you feel *really* good."

The room fell dark and my screams subsided amid the haze of anesthesia . . . amid the fear of a new unknown.

Twenty-Seven

Beep. Beep. Beep. I could hear the steady rhythm of a heart monitor slowly pulling me into consciousness. Where *was* I? I could feel tubes attached to me here, there, and everywhere. I tried repositioning myself to get more comfortable, but the machines wouldn't let me. They kept my body locked where I was. Everything was foggy. Forcing my eyelids open required a hundred times more effort than usual. When I finally got them parted into tiny slits of recognition, my first gaze fell on a deep purple shirt. Unmistakable. It was Mamaw—the most comforting person I could imagine to see. Seeing her in the recovery room made me wish I was in her ugly lounge chair, sitting in her lap, rocking in her arms as I'd done so many times before. Just her and me.

"Where am I?" I said groggily. "What's going on?"

I could tell other people were in the room, but I didn't recognize any of them. Turns out they were representatives from the Department of Child and Family Services. There was Carol, for instance (someone I *didn't* want to see), and she had brought along some additional guests.

People that I couldn't physically *bear* to see.

"I know you won't like this," she said to me, despite catching me in such a vulnerable position, "but I want you to know your parents are here. I think it's important that they see you."

"What?!"

Perhaps never in the history of modern medicine has any patient leaped in a nanosecond through the mists of drug-induced semiconsciousness into wide-awake fury. I started shaking with fear and yanking on cords, fighting to detach and escape from my bed. It was too late. There they were. My mother and father were walking across the room toward me, followed by my big brother, Rilvan.

I was overcome with anger. Terrified. I took one look in my dad's eyes and screamed out, "I forgive you! I forgive you!" The medication was influencing my system, I'm sure, but I didn't know what else to do or say in the moment, even as my mother broke down sobbing, saying, "My baby . . ." Her wailing attracted the attention of the entire hospital floor, so much so that my attorney, Angie Lloyd, waiting outside in the hall, barged into the room.

John Stemberger had found Kort Gotterdam, an Ohio lawyer who was a board-certified criminal defense attorney, and Angie Lloyd, a law professor, to help me after my case had been sent to Ohio. Angie, like Rosa, was a rare expert on child immigration and dependency law. A perfect fit and just as hard a fighter!

"Out! Out! You can't be in here!" Angie normally gets her way in or out of the courtroom, and as usual, her protests accomplished her objective. She escorted my parents firmly but respectfully from the room.

She wasn't so respectful with Carol after she returned to my room.

"Carol, there is a *court order* being violated right now!"

By that time, of course, I'd already sailed into Carol myself. "How *could* you? You're supposed to *protect* me! How *could* you?!" Despite my weary medicinal stupor, I pounded the hospital bed with my fists, even picking up the closest object I could find to throw at her. Fortunately for both of us it was only a pillow. But Angie did the rest, furiously ordering her out.

I'd hardly had a chance to calm down, having been almost to the point of forgetting why I was there, before a doctor stepped into the room and said with grave urgency, perhaps oblivious to the drama playing out, "Rifqa, we need to get you right into surgery. We need to start your anesthesia immediately."

"Huh? What are you talking about?"

Mamaw had been told beforehand. "They need to do something to stop the bleeding, honey, and also to remove the polyp that has been growing inside you."

Everything happened so very fast.

The first procedure apparently had found something potentially terrible: a polyp (whatever that was). I could sense the urgency of the medical team when they conveyed me by wheelchair to another room. They placed me on a black cushioned table under blinding white lights, and then they plastered my body with sticky white cables.

"Relax and think happy thoughts," they said, trying to calm my jangled spirits. "You're in good hands, kiddo." And then, like before, those famous last words: "It's going to be okay, sweetie."

My awareness faded to black for the second time that night.

At home a week later, I fluffed my hair in the bedroom mirror, allowing the fresh curls to gracefully shape my face. Carol was coming over (ugh!), but I was intent on looking my best and staying above her cattiness. Besides, graduation was only a couple of months away, and my eighteenth birthday was a couple of months after that. If I could bide my time with Carol for a short while longer, I could say goodbye to caseworkers for good.

So I strode confidently into the living room to see what she needed to talk about. I sat as far away from her as the rules of etiquette politely allowed and noticed a stack of papers in front of her.

"Rifqa," she said with an air that told me something was wrong, "you have cancer."

I stared for several seconds across the room, lost in a brief daze, and then sort of laughed in disbelief. "No, I don't," I said. "You can't be serious."

She nodded. "The doctors thought at first that the polyp wasn't cancerous, but the biopsy revealed otherwise. I'm so sorry."

She *was* serious.

I had cancer.

"Mamaw?" She reached out to grab my hands, sympathetic tears welling in her eyes. I blinked away at my own tears too, trying hard to support the weight of this staggering news. I'm dying. *I'm dying?* Why was Carol the one to tell me this?

"You have a doctor's appointment in a few hours," she said, "and I wanted you to be prepared."

Carol. Always making independent decisions that were in my "best interest." And always making me wonder what in the world she was thinking.

I grabbed my hair, tugging away at this newest knot of turmoil—much more upset with the horrifying reality of my condition, of course, than with Carol's impertinence. Would I not be able to go to college? Would I not be able to marry? Would I not have any babies? Would I lose more control over my life than I'd already lost?

The doctor, once we reached her office later that day, answered all of these questions with one blow. The tall, dark-skinned Indian woman in the white lab coat stood beside me while I sat on the examination table, and then she sat down, taking my trembling hands in hers.

"Rifqa, I need to tell you the truth, okay? You generously have one year to live, even with the best treatment we can offer."

What!?

Physicians all over the nation would eventually study my case. It was most unusual. Extraordinary. I actually had *two* types of cancer. One of them (rhabdomyosarcoma) was commonly found in young children, while the other (adenocarcinoma) was generally seen only in menopausal women. I was neither, of course. And yet I had both. Taken together, they gave me one of the worst and weirdest forms of uterine cancer anybody had ever seen.

"That's why we would highly suggest," she said, "in addition to chemotherapy, that you submit to a hysterectomy. That means you could
never bear children, of course, but it could only help you. I'm so sorry,
Rifqa."

No one can predict for you how you'll react to such a devastating report. I recognized the gravity of it: my likely death and the short, painful
life between now and then. But in the freshness of that moment, I was in
denial of the prognosis. Death didn't seem like it had beaten me yet. My
main concern, for whatever reason, was the *certainty* that a hysterectomy
would remove all possibility of having a family. Part of my dream, as I'd
battled through the struggles of the past few years, involved being able to
start a new line of Christian believers through my future marriage and
motherhood. I thought of it often. This dull ache of knowledge—the absolute relinquishment of my ability to conceive and bear children—rocked
me to the core of my being.

I fell into Mamaw's arms, drenching her shoulder with tears and sobbing at the prospect of more losses than I could imagine or bear.

Graduation came along in the midst of several surgeries, including one in
which they inserted a port in my chest for chemotherapy treatments.
While I was obviously weak and distracted with life as a cancer patient—
perhaps the ultimate backdrop for both appreciating a great accomplish-
ment as well as keeping it in humble perspective—plans rolled forward
toward the big day.

I was graduating as valedictorian of my class, and some of my favorite
people in the world would be there to celebrate with me. Mamaw and
Papaw, of course, as well as Isabella and Raven, but also Brian and Michaela, and even Rosa who'd flown in from Miami for the festivities. What
a precious moment, despite the sad overtones, as I sat there in my golden

sandals, awaiting the moment when I would walk across the stage, receive my diploma, and then join the others in tossing our red hats into the air in celebration.

But, first, the school district director approached the podium and said,

There may actually be times when making the right choice for yourself as an individual seems to put you at odds with the world. Now, we all know the easy choice could make your life much simpler and less painful, but the easy choice was not the right choice for this young woman. So looking to the God of her understanding for guidance, she chose a path toward her vision of freedom.

Now, this choice had extreme consequences, wreaking havoc on her life. Her home, her security, her serenity, and even her safety were thrown into the madness. Her life became a media whirlwind, and she was overwhelmed by negativity from many sources. She was bombarded with evil messages and with actual death threats. The madness threatened to overtake her and smother the spirit of her soul.

However, this young woman did not succumb to the madness. She found her spark, her special gift, and rose from the wreckage of the madness. . . . She chose an attitude of love despite the pain, an attitude of compassion despite the hate shown her, an attitude of perseverance. . . . At only seventeen years old, she found the strength to overcome the madness and succeed.

She has maintained a Focus Grade Point Average of 4.16 while earning 9.5 credits in less than six months. She was also recently diagnosed with a life-threatening illness. Despite going through surgery on Thursday of last week to remove the cancer, she was at graduation rehearsal on Tuesday of this week with a smile on her face. And despite all the hate that has been thrown at her, and despite all the evil she has seen, she is determined to one day travel and minister to those who are less fortunate.

Me.

She was talking about *me.*

I couldn't believe it. I felt so humble and small, walking forward to receive a special award from the board of directors. As deep as the pain had descended into my heart, the amount of joy that flooded my soul in that moment was greater than almost any other I'd ever experienced. More than the applause of the audience, I could feel the tangible, weighty honor of my heavenly Father, encircling me in love, grace, and acceptance.

I didn't know what was coming next, of course. Like always. Though I guess I *did* know what was coming, at least to hear the doctors tell it.

Maybe God and I had a few tricks up our sleeves that could change all that.

Twenty-Eight

I always hated being cooped up inside or in classes throughout the summers of my childhood. Those were such long, unbearable, unhappy days, yet maybe not as bad as being strapped to heart monitors, injected with chemo treatments, feeling deathly sick under the pretense of being made well and kept comfortable.

This was not how I expected to spend the final summer of my adolescence.

Life a long time ago had ceased being easy and expected for me. I'd grown to accept that. The Lord had caused my faith in Him to be a fight from the very start of my conversion. Apathy was not in my vocabulary. And while I did wrestle, I admit, with deep groans of depression and self-pity through some of these physically, emotionally, spiritually demanding days, I tried as hard as possible to maintain an essence of joy through it all.

My foster family helped. I remember a time when Mamaw was driving me home from a chemo session, letting me listen to Christian radio in the car. (What a freedom from what I'd experienced growing up or even in other foster homes.) JJ Heller's "Your Hands" began playing, how "when my world is shaking . . . I never leave Your hands," and I cranked the volume to match the volume of my own voice, belting out my worship alongside the recording artist and with unabashed confidence in Jesus.

Mamaw and I cried. We praised Him. I told her I wasn't afraid to die. She told me she wasn't ready to let me go. Together we shared the fellowship of suffering against the light of God's heavenly hope while the sun radiated its warmth through the windshield and we battled every foe that threatened to deaden and destroy me.

Another day, not long afterward, while sitting with eyes closed through a treatment at the hospital, I turned toward a sound of movement in the room and spied Isabella with a large straw hat in one hand and an unopened can of orange soda in the other.

I rested my head back with a weary smile and uttered softly, "Isabella, thank you."

She knew my weakness for orange pop. And the hat was a sweet, almost forgotten memory. We had been out shopping months before when I'd snatched this ridiculously large hat off the rack and said, "Hey, Isabella, look at this one!" I plopped it on my head and made a kissing face. She instinctively grabbed one that was like it and flashed a diva pose, hands on hips. Mamaw, the typical mother, snapped pictures on her phone to capture the moment.

And now, as a tangible way to try to silently say how much they loved me, they had gone back to the store to buy this straw hat for me, to help keep my mind on happy times.

I ached to hold Isabella and tell her I was okay, but it was hard to speak because of the pain I was experiencing. She squeezed my hand and left the room, breaking out in sobs, and left behind such a swell of gratitude in my heart for a family that truly loved me.

I hated that they were watching me suffer. Sometimes the pain itself wasn't as bad as seeing them hurting. I worried about how my ongoing ordeal was affecting them, especially the girls. One day while Isabella was sitting with me at the hospital, trying not to be upset, I asked her if she'd write down what she was thinking and feeling. "That's always been healing for me," I told her. I couldn't believe, though, the depth of awareness and questions in her words when I read them later. I'll share them with you in all their childlike, ungrammatical honesty:

Today I saw the scariest thing. I went to the hospital with my sister
Riffy. She was having chemo put into her port and we were sitting

here clowning. The doctor came in and was describing stuff to her and I was just sitting here acting like it don't bother me. Then we went to a different room and they lifted up her shirt and put this cream on where the port was so it wouldn't hurt so bad. I was thinking to myself what if that was me? Then they came in with the chemo. That was the really scary part. I was just looking into her eyes and seeing the fear and seeing the light of Jesus gleam into her eyes. She held my hand, and it was just so scary. I will not stop thinking about this until the day that I die. I have so many questions. Why does she have to go through all of this pain?

I certainly wasn't beyond asking that question myself, many times, most especially, maybe, when I began losing all my hair. I would be in the shower, and a large clump of it would just wad up in my hands as I was washing it. It started shedding everywhere, anywhere, all the time. Gross. Embarrassing.

One rainy night, as the thunder and lightning echoed through the house, I begged Mamaw to take me someplace where I could get it all cut off, shaved bald. I was sick of this.

"Well, honey, it's late, it's raining, and it's Sunday. All the salons are closed."

"I don't care. I can't deal with it anymore!"

"Okay, well, I do know a lady who runs a salon out of her basement. If you'll call her, and if she'll see you, I'll take you there."

I was desperate enough to do it. Mamaw gave me the lady's number. When I told her the situation, she said yes immediately.

Not too many hours later I sat in front of a stranger's mirror, watching with odd, almost fascinated disbelief as she razored every bit of hair from my head. Days would come later when I'd stare into a mirror and gasp at what I saw. Swollen pink eyelids. The pale, skinny face. I looked like a ghost. With my blind eye and bald head, I felt like a freak. Deformed. I wished on some mornings, countless mornings, that I would fall asleep and never wake up. Running my hands over my bald, fleshy head in the early darkness, I wanted to crawl in a hole and hide from the world. Every seventeen-year-old I wanted to be like was at home, on vacation, or off on a summer mission trip in some part of the world. They were either preparing for their ACTs, planning their college classes for the fall, shopping, or laughing and talking into the wee hours with their friends. I, on the other hand, having escaped one death threat only to run head-on into another one, was looking at the last, fading, whimpering few months of a life that seemed not only un-fun but altogether unfair.

In the basement of this kind woman's house on a rainy night in Ohio, looking for the first time at my brown bald head, I made a deal with God. "You know, Lord, the Bible says a woman's hair is her glory. Well, I am laying down my glory tonight, all my strength and my beauty, for Yours." I paused in my thoughts as the weight of this truth consumed me.

"And when it grows back," I said to myself in utter, undeniable faith, "will You let it be more beautiful than it was before?"

I'd been pacing the floor, rehearsing just how I was going to say this. Six to eight weeks of cancer treatments had weakened me to the point where I wondered which was worse: dying or having your insides killed in order to live.

Mamaw was on the phone as I entered the living room. My fidgeting and nervousness captured her attention, and she told the person on the other end of the call that she would have to call her back. After hanging up, she asked, "What do you need, honey?"

"I, um . . . I, uh . . ."

"What is it, Rifqa?"

"I'm stopping the treatments."

"You're *what*?" she said, snatching the glasses from her face as she leaned forward to the edge of her chair, becoming the first of several people to declare me insane for this rash, illogical conclusion. This included my oncologist, of course, who looked me straight in the eye, trying to convince me with his solemn countenance.

"Rifqa, dear, do you realize what you're doing? You are going to *die* if you go through with this."

I wouldn't be moved. I'd decided. I was dying anyway. What the cancer wasn't doing, the chemo was. The path I needed to walk had become— I don't know how to describe it exactly—very clear to me. And chemotherapy wasn't part of it.

I knew it sounded crazy. *Was* crazy. It didn't make sense to me either. But I knew in my spirit that God was calling me to do this, and I decided I would rather die in obedience to Him than live in disobedience and possibly survive the treatment. The same whisper that lifted me up from my hiding place that Sunday morning behind a tree at my parents' apartments was the same voice that asked me to do something everybody in my life protested. It was saying the same thing as before.

By faith, Rifqa . . . By faith . . .

I wasn't going through with the hysterectomy, and I wasn't going through with any more chemo treatments. The doctors had removed whatever they'd been able to remove in surgery, and God would take care of the rest by healing me. Otherwise I would die. But my life was not my own anymore, and my spirit found a way to be at rest with that. I would serve Him with joy for however much longer He allowed me to live, and I would love Him to the absolute fullest even if these were my last months on earth.

Twenty-Nine

As much safety and shelter as my foster family's home had provided, even through my unexpected ordeal with cancer, it still hadn't been able to keep the reality of my legal situation completely at bay. Although my parents and their original attorneys had accepted without much protest the ruling of the Florida judge, they changed course once I was back on Ohio soil. Despite the fact that everyone had agreed to settle (1) by sending me back to Ohio with the condition of keeping me in state custody (foster care) and (2) by ensuring I received my legal immigration status, matters refused to stay as simple as that.

Shortly after I arrived in Mamaw and Papaw's home, my parents hired new Islamic attorneys to fight the order and have me returned into their custody. While this parade of appeals trailed clumsily along, resulting in more and more hearings and crazy courtroom proceedings over the next year, I tried to stay focused on school and enjoy what little relief and freedom I had. All the while, my parents steadfastly denied abusing me or threatening me and claimed they just wanted me to come home. To an outsider, they might've sounded convincing. I, however, knew the truth. I knew I could never go back to them.

I clung to the fact that I was about to become an adult in the eyes of the law. Once I reached my eighteenth birthday, I would be emancipated by the state of Ohio, and my case would be closed. That legal drama would be over. I could never be returned to my family's custody and never be sent back to Sri Lanka against my will.

It was a dream come true, walking out of the courtroom on my eighteenth birthday. Miraculously my green card had been granted by the federal government the day before. I was with Angie when she called John and Rosa to announce the good news about my immigration status. We all yelped screams of delight, and Angie and I jumped up and down in celebration. Because of the juvenile provision that made me eligible for it, I wouldn't have been able to apply beyond my eighteenth birthday. So we were taken down to the absolute wire. But my immigration status was finally permanent.

My parents also dropped their threat of taking me to court as an "unruly child." Had they kept it up, my eighteenth birthday wouldn't have changed much. I could have been forced to be a defendant against their charges. They must have realized, however, that if they persisted in this scorched-earth approach, every detail of our home and family life would go shockingly public. Then, instead of it quenching their thirst for recapturing and attaining honor in the community, it would have severed what little remained of it. Our relationship would've gone from nothing to less than nothing. So even though a trial date was set at one point, and my legal team prepared for a hearing, my parents eventually retreated.

It was over.

Everything was over.

I was free.

From the corner of my eye, I saw my family gathering their things and exiting the courtroom. My older brother was leaning against a bench, waiting, perhaps wondering what was next. My heart seized at the sight of him, aching to embrace him and comfort him. He looked so broken and pained.

I thought back to the last time he and I had spoken, during a supervised meeting in Florida. "I'm sorry for what I did to your eye," he told me that day, uncharacteristically tearing up. I looked into his watery brown eyes, feeling my own heart gushing with compassion for him at the genuine guilt written across his face. We were sitting at a pale wooden table next to a window. Rays of light hovered over us, catching wisps of dust in the streaming glow.

I cupped my brother's face in my hands and whispered in deepest earnestness, "Look at me. I forgive you. It's okay." We both sat there, staring at each other through our tears.

"Rifqa," he said, trying to cut through it all, "please come home. Please! Everything can be forgotten. You can practice your Christianity. Everything can go back to the way we were."

"I'm sorry, Rilvan, I can't. It's not easy like that."

We both knew it. *I* knew it at least. But I held his hands in mine as we spoke, baptized in the anguish of what we both wished were true. A few minutes later our brief meeting was forced to end, and I held on to him, not wanting him to walk away but realizing he must, aching that I was leaving not only my family behind me but a part of my heart as well.

This fact was never more clear than in that final moment in the courtroom on my eighteenth birthday—the end of so much heartbreak, loss, and nail-biting fear overshadowed somehow by the captivating presence of God and the overseeing assurance of His sovereignty.

Yes, I was leaving a lot behind, not only my family, despite their resistance to my Christian faith, but also a lot of my support system, as well as some of the focus that had grown up around me as my determined quest for freedom became a legal battle for justice. As a result of winning our hard-fought case, it was time for me to hand Angie, John, and Rosa back over to other clients who were in need of their heroic services. It was also time for me to step out on my own, away from Mamaw and Papaw's home—the one generous blessing for which I will forever be grateful to the Ohio foster care system.

It was time for me to go.

But I was leaving to go . . . where?

Since the reality of my teenage life had forced me to keep people at arm's length for so long, I couldn't seamlessly fall back into the nucleus of friends from my past, not without the natural rhythm of school to keep us together. I couldn't just catch a bus to Columbus and hang out so closely to my parents. Besides, my father had used information from my cell phone bill to track down the phone numbers of many of the Christian friends who'd given me so much love and backing through the years. A number of them told me later that he had harassed them, threatening them with police action and prosecution. Even people who cared about me had good reason to avoid me. They had understandably moved on.

It was time for me to move on too.

And I have. I've now been on my own for five years.

Oddly enough, the legal ordeal has given me inspiration to explore the possibilities of going into law. Most of my life, I have lived as the one oppressed and victimized. As I write my story for you, I realize that I have an unquenchable desire to fight for the voiceless and oppressed. Through my own experience, I have gained a passion for justice that has not left me. Ultimately, I know it is God who executes true justice. There is no judicial system that can restore to me everything I have lost; it is God who avenges.

I wish I knew, but I really am not sure what that is going to look like. For now, I am taking my passion and pouring myself into my college studies in philosophy and politics.

I don't know what will ever become of my relationship with my parents and family. It's hard to see anything approaching reconciliation unless they come to know Jesus and are able to discover, by the same grace that reached out to me, why He is what life is all about. Worth every risk. Worth every sacrifice.

I can't help but wonder, though.

Almost every brown-skinned Asian boy I see reminds me of my baby brother, Rajaa. When one near his age happened to wander over to the buffet line at an Indian restaurant where a friend and I were eating recently, I dropped my dish and burst into sobs. In that moment it was as if all the breath in my lungs had vanished and time stopped moving. While I was kneeling on the floor to collect myself and my fallen dinnerware, the question hit me: How different would life look if I was still in little Rajaa's life? As time has passed, I've seen how much of a part he plays in the tremendous grief I still feel. Whatever happens, I'll never get back those years of his childhood that I've missed. I may never see him again, and I don't know how to calculate that cost. I just know it never stops adding up.

I still have passing dreams where I see my mother, with gray streaks in her dark curly hair, cutting up chicken for curry. I want to hold her and tell her about Jesus, to tell her I'm safe. But then she's gone, locked away from me, the hardness never leaving her eyes, even in memory.

And then my father, what can I say? I can never erase the memories. Most of them I want to forget, to recoil and run away from as fast and as far as I can. They still possess the power to frighten and terrify me, even from a distance.

I can say now, though, through all of it, that I look back today and see reasons for being grateful to him. He fed me and put a roof over my head for sixteen years. He worked hard to support us and cared about my education. Mainly, though, I register with Joseph's story from the Old Testament, who chose by necessity and survival to go on his way and put the past behind him. He even named his firstborn son a word meaning "forget," wanting to "forget all my toil and all my father's house" (Genesis 41:51). And while God seems to confirm to me that one day, in some way, we will experience a reconciliation of sorts, it will need to be like Joseph's with his father and family, miraculous in every detail. Still I pray for it, just as I pray for every one of them, just as I've done since I was twelve years old, though never more incessantly than I pray for them today.

I do forgive my father, even though I fail to understand him—just as perhaps you fail to understand me. Not everyone's story can be laid over everyone else's and used as a grid or template for determining how a person is supposed to react. Here's what you must know if you want to understand: Not only did I leave Islam, but I shamed my family. And this shame is of a category and description that goes beyond the ability of most people to relate to if they're unfamiliar with strict Muslim law and culture. Those who *do* understand it, and understand it very well, are those who have wanted me dead. That's why I have taken, and continue to take, precautions to protect my life and safety.

Forgiveness, by its nature, must often go into very hard places. I know. I've gone there. But forgiveness is not foolish and blind, an unthinking make-nice. Wisdom sometimes must tell even people who've genuinely forgiven to take ongoing steps that are hard to implement and apply and which to others may not look very forgiving. The heart of forgiveness can't be judged in black-and-white, cookie-cutter dimensions that work fine in a spiritual lab but not in real life.

I love my parents and want their ultimate good wholeheartedly, passionately. I've knelt with my friend Brian on the same patch of ground where I hid from my parents outside our old apartment complex and prayed for my family's salvation. I've traced my fingers along the tree trunk, still able to vividly recall each thought and emotion that drove me there and drove me on. I want to forget. But I can't ever forget.

I've concluded in these past years that God has His reasons for why He won't let me forget. One of them is to say to my many sisters born in Islam that there is more to life than the burdensome guilt and drudgery imposed on them by the religion we've shared. Jesus is freedom and forgiveness, hope and love, peace and purpose, plain and simple.

Another reason is to stand up everywhere oppression is found and encourage the voiceless who labor under the cruel taskmaster of injustice. I pray that my story testifies to the power of God's prevailing against the forces of darkness and how even one person driven to follow Him is enough to cause nations and governments to quail in response. When united as brothers and sisters in Christ, we can truly move mountains.

And if for no other reason, I deem it a privilege to carry my cross with all men and women across the globe who have paid and are paying a high price for declaring Jesus as Lord. I am not the only one; I am one of untold numbers who live in hiding for His name yet are honored to walk in His footsteps and exalt His name by forsaking all to follow Him. Wherever the church has lost this passion and fervor, may stories like mine disturb the cobwebs that limit believers' faith to a menu selection—when Jesus is truly the feast Himself. If you are drawn toward a renewed wholeheartedness to Christ in reading some of my story, may God alone be praised. He is worthy.

I live today in spiritual freedom, able to worship Jesus without restraint or apology.

I live today in physical freedom, having been declared after repeated tests and exams to be free of cancer by no other explanation than the healing finger of almighty God.

I live today in mental, emotional, and relational freedom, having seen the words of Scripture proven true that say, "Everyone who has left houses or brothers or sisters or father or mother or children or lands, for My name's sake, shall receive a hundredfold" (Matthew 19:29). God has brought men and women into my life who love me dearly and would give their own lives to protect me.

I may be in hiding.

But I am hiding in the light.

Discussion Questions

1. What were your expectations for *Hiding in the Light* before you began reading? What image did you have of the author, knowing only the basic idea of her story?

2. Rifqa felt oppressed by her parents both because she was a female and because she had a physical blemish (her damaged eye). She compared herself to a stray kitten: "Dirty. Devalued. Unclean" (page 11). Describe a time when you have felt oppressed or shut out.

3. During Rifqa's early years, her family and culture affected her view of God in a profound way. How is that similar to or different from the way your family and culture have influenced your view of God?

4. Several Christians whom Rifqa met after moving to the United States, including her friends Aiden and Angela, attracted her to Jesus because of the way they treated others and the way they talked about God. Why do you think such words or actions are powerful? Do you think most Christians today believe they can have that kind of effect on a non-Christian? Why or why not?

5. With the encouragement of several Christians, Rifqa found herself "inching deeper and deeper into the ocean of God's unconditional love and truth" (page 59). Which statement below comes closest to your view about evangelizing people of other faiths? Why?

- I don't think we should do it. As long as they believe in God in some form, they're fine the way they are, and we might do more harm than good.
- They're lost without Jesus, so we need to share the gospel with them sensitively yet boldly.
- We should pray for them and trust that we will be the aroma of Christ in their lives, but we don't need to directly talk with them about God.

6. For three years after beginning to follow Jesus, Rifqa hid her new faith from her family and continued to practice the Islamic rituals when she was required to. Do you think Rifqa made a wise choice in hiding her faith or do you feel she was compromising her new beliefs? Why?

7. In a situation like Rifqa's, how do you reconcile the fifth commandment to honor your mother and father with the biblical commandment to live out your faith?

8. Rifqa's father threatened to kill her. Her mother said they were going to take her back to Sri Lanka and commit her to an asylum. Given the family dynamics, do you take these threats at face value or do you think Rifqa may have misinterpreted or overreacted to what was going on? Explain your opinion.

9. Imagine discovering that your child has converted to Islam or some other faith. How would you react in that situation?

10. Based on Rifqa's story, what are some generalizations about Muslims you think are safe to make and some generalizations about Muslims that are *not* safe to make?

11. Rather than renounce Christ, Rifqa left her home in the middle of the night and never returned. What's the boldest move you've made in an attempt to be faithful to Christ?

12. Brian, Beverly, and others aided the teenaged Rifqa in her plan to run away from her parents even though technically they might've been committing a crime by doing so. Did they make the right choices? What would you have done in their place?

13. Rifqa sensed a profound presence of God at certain key moments in her life's journey, such as shortly after she ran away from home and when she was confined in a juvenile detention center in Florida. Describe a time when you felt the undeniable presence of God and what it meant to you.

14. The authorities in Florida eventually decided to send Rifqa back to Ohio on the condition that she not be returned to her family. Rifqa was placed in the foster care system until she turned eighteen. Do you believe the courts made the best decision? Why or why not?

15. Rifqa's court case created debates all over the world. Some people said that it exposed the dangers of Islam. Others claimed that it revealed the unfounded hysteria Christians have about Muslims. What do you think are the lessons of Rifqa's case?

16. In the midst of her hardships while trying to worship Christ in freedom, Rifqa faced another awful trial: a diagnosis of terminal cancer. What part do you think the experience with cancer played in her spiritual development?

17. At the end of the book, Rifqa says that she tells her story for three reasons:
    - To say to others who are oppressed under Islam that there is freedom and hope in Jesus.
    - To encourage those who are struggling against injustice of any sort that it's possible to be victorious.
    - To remind readers of the men and women all around the world who are paying a high price for declaring Jesus as Lord.

    How did her story change your views of those struggling against injustice? What can you do to help the oppressed and persecuted?

18. Describe what it means to you to have freedom through Christ.

19. If you could ask Rifqa anything, what would you ask her?

20. What do you think the phrase "hiding in the light" means in the context of this book?

21. What is one way you came to understand God more through reading Rifqa's story?

22. We don't have the luxury of choosing our own ending to Rifqa's story. She is still in hiding and possibly still in danger. What does this lack of resolution suggest about how God works in our lives?

Acknowledgments

To my editor: You and I both know this book would not be what it is without your precious time devoted to these words. Thank you for being the coach I desperately needed. The lives that will be touched and the hearts that are turned toward Christ are a direct result of the time you gave to my story. Thank you.

To my agent, Robert Wolgemuth: Papa Robert, I adore you. I love how you have fathered me through this entire process by zealously guarding my story and my heart. You have treated me more like a daughter than a client! I pray and dream that one day I could be loved by a man the same way that you loved Bobbie.

To Brian Williams, and to Blake and Beverly Lorenz, the key players of my story: Thank you for risking your life, reputation, and future for the sake of righteousness. Without your courageous risk in my story, there would be no story to tell. You are a gift to me!

To John Stemberger, one of my heroes: I was a client who could give you no money in return but required all your time, energy, and resources. You lost more than you gained in representing me. It took from your family life and your own financial status, and it even put your health at risk. Yet the entire way you were a rock, praising Him and encouraging me the entire way. Thank you for being my big brother and being willing to still be in my life when all the cameras faded away. I aspire to follow in your footsteps and fight crime just like you when I grow up one day.

To my best friend and "Jonathan": You know who you are! Thank you for loving me like Christ. You were there on those days when I wasn't so brave. Those days when all I could do was be angry as I cried out to God, sitting in agony and asking over and over again, "Why?" You grieved with me in the silence and waited patiently for me to heal. Thank you for carrying me when I became crippled and could no longer keep going. Thank you for loving me in my most unlovable moments. My dearest sister, I cannot wait for the memories that will be created as we run the race set before us together, striving to make Christ our greatest treasure and possession. I love you.